ART OF THE FLY

ART OF THE FLY

How to tie flies for fishing fresh and salt waters

FRANK O'LEARY

VIKING
an imprint of
PENGUIN BOOKS

Contents

A note about hooks and fly sizes

Hooks for fly-tying are available in a wide range of configurations, which allows you to select the hook best suited to a particular pattern.

With freshwater (trout) hooks, gauge and length are the usual variations; they may be described as '1 x extra-fine' or '2 x short', for example. Hook eyes may be nominated as 'up' or 'down', and the hook gape may also vary. Hooks are usually straight, but shrimp and pupa hooks have a curved shank for a more realistic tie.

For trout patterns, the proportions are based around the hook size. The following dimensions may be used as a guide:

- tail – approximately 1–1½ times the hook length

- body – approximately ⅔ of the hook length

- wing – same length as hook shank

- hackle – approximately 1–1½ times the hook gape

Saltwater hooks and patterns are larger and more robust; in most cases, proportions vary from one pattern to the next, and often they will be based on the pattern itself, not the hook size. For example, Mcvay's Gotcha has a tail the same length as the hook shank, and the wing extends to the end of the tail or twice the hook length. Many other saltwater patterns, such as the Surf Candy, can be trimmed to shape at the vice or to match the bait when fishing. The final shape and length are really up to you.

Introduction

My introduction to fly tying came about quite by chance. My early days were spent on Victorian rivers like the Goulburn, and my fly box was full of all sorts of patterns that were allegedly high on the trouts' menu that particular day.

Before long a new box was acquired to house more new flies, and things got complicated as the collection grew. Fishing is rarely straightforward and fly fishing can turn the straightest of paths into a meandering expedition through seemingly endless possibilities. Often, as our quarry snubbed our offerings (were there even any fish there?), the fallback position of a Bead-head Flashback Nymph fished in tandem with an Elk-hair Caddis was the undoing of more than the occasional trout. We regained our composure, muttered something about the fish being taken on the nymph and walked on to next likely hotspot.

A little more science might have straightened our path. But, as is the case for many fly-fisherman, busy working lives meant trips were all too infrequent and, as a result, the lessons learned were hazy memories by the time of the next foray. Instead, information was sought and gathered on what the fish were targeting this week; boxes were duly checked for missing parts of the puzzle, and off we'd go.

Despite this superficial understanding of life in the subaquatic world, we managed to snag enough fish to want to do it all over again – a bit like the weekend golfer who finds the sweet spot once in 120 swings. Incrementally, though, our knowledge was growing and we began to understand a little more about how that caddis came to hatch and what that nymph was doing there. It was still a bit hit-and-miss, but at least our patterns were underpinned by a modicum of theory.

Some years later, on a trip to Victoria's High Country, I was pressing our host and local fly-fisherman for information on where to fish and which fly might do the trick, as my wife plotted my demise from our room. Fly-fishermen being the friendly folk they are, especially to fellow devotees, I was soon armed with enough information to write a pocket guidebook for the area. But they make some decent wine in that neck of the woods, and the next morning the idea of a guidebook was a distant memory at the bottom of an empty glass.

All was not lost, however. We had agreed to spend the day on the Howqua River and our host delivered more than a reviving breakfast: some time between the muesli and the bacon and eggs, I was handed a small dry fly and told, 'Here you go, this is what you need'. Itching to try out the fly, I tied it on and started making my way upstream. I came to a bend in the river that had that nice combination of a fast run flanked by a deeper eddy, and was worthy of a cast. I was standing in thigh-deep water, downstream and in the centre of the river, when I made my cast. I had avoided the trees on my back cast and landed the fly in the mid-section of the run; it skated off onto the eddy and was immediately taken – so fast that I didn't have time to react, and before I knew it, the fish was careering downstream, swimming straight past me. Whether, it was due to the muesli or the bacon and eggs, I regained my composure pretty quickly and landed that feisty little rainbow. Unlike so many other great moments in history, there was no one to witness this 'one cast, one fish' start to the day.

So here I was, somewhere on the Howqua, having received spiritual enlightenment. There was more to the game than just throwing flies at fish: fly-fishing is not so much how you deliver the flies, but what you deliver. Tying flies gives you the opportunity to tweak existing patterns or, better still, to create your own, and that day I experienced at first hand how effective and satisfying this could be. Not long after, I started tying my own flies.

When first approached to do this book, I gave little thought to the complexities of the project, but rather greeted the opportunity with all the fervour of a new chum.

Eventually I realised the enormity of the task of selecting 25 freshwater flies and 25 saltwater ones. Most fly-fisherman will have their 'go-to' fly – the one that puts the runs on the board when all else fails – and a quick browse through a number of publications suggested that there are many personalised favourites out there. So, rather than selecting a group of flies that might only be known to their creators and those lucky enough to have access to his/her fly box, I decided to focus on the more common flies and proven fish-takers, which – In theory at least – should equip an angler with enough patterns to fill the box and to cover most fishing situations.

Where possible I've acknowledged the fly's creator, but some flies (such as buzzers and emergers) have evolved into a tying style rather than a specific pattern. This doesn't make things any easier, though, as there are many variations of the same style and many of them are very similar. So I would encourage you to explore and experiment to determine what bests fits the bill for your situation.

This book is really a celebration of the fly, both as a way of catching fish and as an age-old technique. It is not designed to be a definitive guide, and to that end the recipes provide easy-to-follow steps without listing every possible hook or material option. Exploring and experimenting is what fly tying is all about.

It would be remiss of me not to thank a few people. Mick Kaksa for advice and supplies, and the following tyers who very generously provided information on their patterns and gave approval for inclusion of their fly: Craig Worthington, Muz Wilson, Mick Winterton, Ken Culgin, Rob Laspina.

FRANK O'LEARY
September 2008

Anchovy Bomb

As its name might suggest, this pattern was designed to replicate an anchovy. After observing a large run of anchovies enter The Bay of Islands in New Zealand, an area rich in marine life, it was obvious to the fly's creator, Craig Worthington, that if his flies were to be noticed they would need to mimic the fluid movement of the fish; pearl Polar Flash proved to be the perfect material. The fly proved to be the undoing of many fish on its first outing, catching fish as fast as it could be recast. Since then, the Anchovy Bomb has accounted for many species ranging from kingfish and snapper in New Zealand to queenfish at Weipa on Cape York Peninsula in far north-eastern Australia.

It's important that the sink rate of this fly be quicker than that of the line, in order to avoid tangles. Using the largest dumbbell eyes possible, wrapping the shank of the hook with lead wire or copper wire, and finishing the fly with epoxy will help eliminate this problem, as will tying the Polar Flash across the top of the eyes and parallel to the hook.

This fly is best fished with a shooting head such as T-14. Once cast, allow it to sink and then retrieve it with a long, loping movement (or flat-out, for the likes of queenfish).

Materials

Hook	Gamakatsu SL12S, sizes 2/0–6/0	Weight	Heavy copper wire
		Wing	Pearl Polar Flash
Thread	Flat waxed nylon	Body	Silver tinsel, finished with epoxy
Eyes	Large dumbbell		

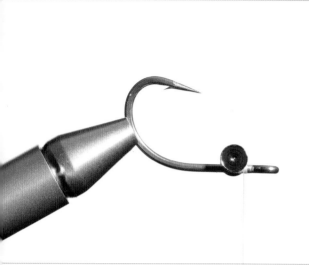
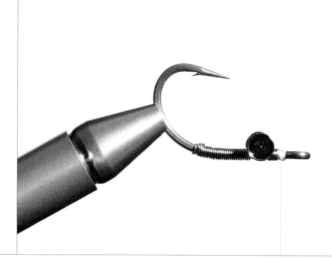

Step 1

Tie in the dumbbell eyes on the same side of the hook as the gape, making sure to leave enough room for tying off the wing materials and forming the head.

Step 2

Tie in a short piece of copper wire at the bend of the hook, and wrap over and around eyes to form a short, weighted body.

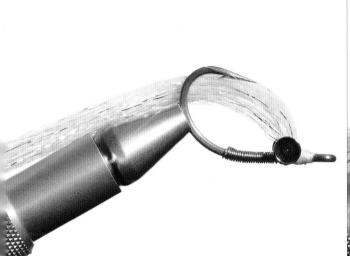 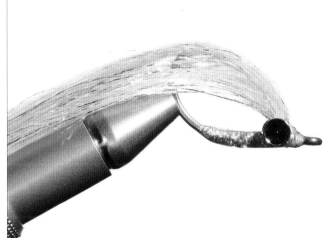

Step 3

Tie in a bunch of Polar Flash that is two or three times longer than the hook. Make sure it is tied in front of and over the eyes, not behind them. The Polar Flash should sit parallel to the hook shank.

Step 4

Tie in the tinsel and wrap it down to the hook bend and back again, over the eyes, to the front of the hook. Tie off, and coat the whole thing with epoxy.

Baited Breath

Originally tied by US angler and writer Robert McCurdy as a bonefish pattern, the Baited Breath has become popular amongst Australian anglers as anything but a bonefish fly. Instead, it has accounted for many estuarine species (such as flathead and bream) in the south, whilst in the tropics it has caught flats fish such as golden trevally.

The simplicity of the pattern and the materials makes it easy to change the size and colour of this fly to suit local conditions. Try tying purple and black combinations for bream, and tan for the northern flats species; olive is a safe option for all species as a shrimp imitation. Bead-chain eyes are the norm, but heavier eyes may be needed to sink this fly to the bottom for the likes of flathead or golden trevally. If fish can be seen on the flats, cast in front of them and give the fly a couple of twitches to raise a puff of sand or two.

Materials

Hook	Gamakatsu SS15 or Mustad C68SS, sizes 6–1/0	Antennae	Pearl Krystal Flash
		Body	Variegated chenille
Thread	Flat waxed nylon	Eyes	Bead chain
Tail	Marabou feathers and grizzly hackle		

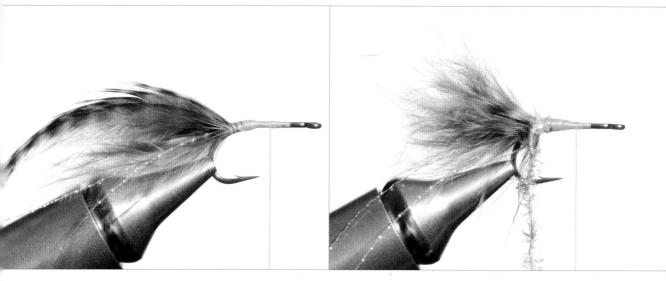

Step 1

Tie in two pieces of marabou, and the
Krystal Flash. Tie in a grizzly hackle at the
base of the marabou.

Step 2

Wind the hackle around the hook three
times and then tie off. Expose the core
of the chenille by pulling away the outer
layer, and tie this end to the hook.

Step 3

Tie in the eyes. Once they are secure, advance the thread to just behind the hook eye.

Step 4

Wrap the hook with the chenille, including around the eyes, and continue wrapping to the hook eye. Tie off the chenille, form a small head, whip-finish, and add a drop of head cement.

Bass Vampire

The Bass Vampire was designed by Queensland angler John Schofield, for use in that state's bass-fishing tournaments. Earlier versions of a similar fly called the Bream Buster, by Des Welch, are thought to have influenced the Vampire. Bass can tend to hang deep, and fishing for them at depths of more than 10 metres is not uncommon. Using a sinking line and glow-in-the-dark dumbbell eyes, Schofield enjoyed great success with this fly and it soon became a popular pattern in other parts of Australia.

Estuarine species such as bream will readily take the Vampire, and it can be deadly when fished around wharves and given lighter-weight eyes so that it sinks slowly. Purple and black have proved to be a killer colour combination for this fly, so why change it?

Materials

Hook	Gamakatsu SS15 or Mustad C68S-SS, sizes 6–1	Eyes	Real Eyes with 3-mm stick-on Glow Eyes
Thread	Flat waxed nylon	Wing	Purple slinky fibre
Tail	Pearl Mylar	Overwing	Black slinky fibre
Body	Black chenille		

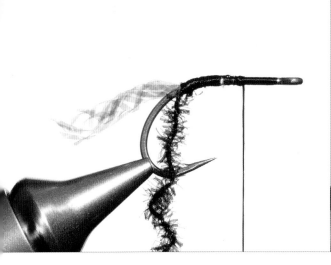 

Step 1

Tie in the Mylar tail, which should be about the length of the hook. Then tie in the chenille.

Step 2

Advance the thread, and tie in the eyes.

Step 3

Wrap the hook with the chenille up to, and once over, the eyes, then tie off.

Step 4

Invert the hook, and tie in the wing.

continued >

Step 5

Tie in the overwing, form a small head, and whip-finish. Complete the fly with a drop of head cement. Apply the stick-on eyes to the Real Eyes, using super glue.

Bead-head Pheasant Tail Flashback Nymph

Frank Sawyer was a river-keeper on the Avon River in Wiltshire for much of his life and created the Pheasant Tail Nymph to imitate members of the Baetis genus of mayflies. His creations were simple affairs, using only pheasant-tail fibres and copper wire, but proved effective around the world and spawned variations to suit local conditions. One of these is the Flashback Nymph, which uses flash for the wing case and peacock herl for the thorax, with a bead head for extra weight. If even more weight is required, tie in lead wire about two-thirds of the way along the hook shank and then wind it along the shank to the bead.

The weight required will be determined by the depth and flow of the water being fished, and can easily be altered by using more or less wire (or, if preferred, a tungsten bead head in lieu of copper). This fly can be fished alone as a searching pattern when surface activity is non-existent, or coupled with a dry as a tandem rig early in the season when the choice between dry or wet is unclear.

Materials

Hook	Tiemco TMC3761 or Kamasan B175, sizes 12–18	Rib	Copper wire
		Body	Pheasant tail
Thread	Dark brown 6/0	Wing case	Flashabou
Head	2-mm copper or gold bead	Thorax	Peacock herl
Tail	Pheasant tail		

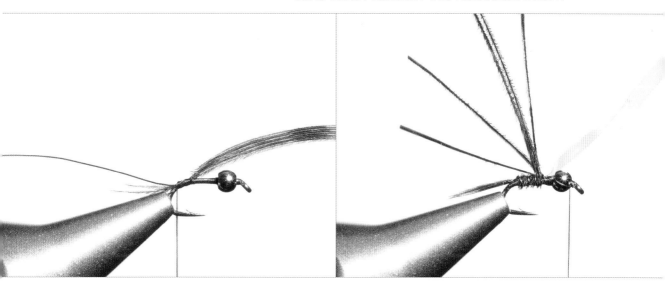

Step 1

Slide the bead onto the hook. For the tail, tie in four pheasant-tail fibres on the top of the hook so the tips protrude past the bend. Next tie in a short piece of copper wire at the tie-in point of the tail. Wind the thread two-thirds of the way towards the hook eye.

Step 2

Wind the pheasant-tail fibres along the hook shank until they meet the thread. Tie off, but don't trim them yet. Now wind the copper wire evenly in the opposite direction to the tail fibres, then tie off and trim. Tie in a small piece of Flashabou.

continued >

Step 3

Select a piece of peacock herl and tie in against the end of the Flashabou to form the thorax. Tie off behind the bead. Bring the ends of the pheasant-tail fibres over the top of the thorax, tie off, and repeat with the Flashabou.

BMS (Bullen Merri Special)

From the vice of Muz Wilson, one of Australia's top fly-tyers, this fly has become a household name. It was created to imitate the smelt of Lake Bullen Merri in western Victoria and as such has also achieved considerable success in Tasmania and New Zealand, which generated a range of flies for fish as wide-ranging as trout and tuna.

Early versions of this pattern used synthetic living fibre (SLF), which had to be put through a grinder to produce dubbing fibre. Muz worked closely with local manufacturer Tiewell to produce an easier alternative, which is available in a range of colours, allowing the angler to tie patterns with a natural translucency. White or grey are standards and are used in both fresh and saltwater, whilst colours such as olive can be useful in weedy areas. If smelters can be seen, cast in front of them and strip the fly through their path.

Materials

Hook	TMC 5262 or Black Magic J8, sizes 8–10	Tail	SLF fibres
		Rib	Silver Mylar
Thread	White 3/0	Body	SLF dubbing
Head	Glass bead	Collar	Red thread

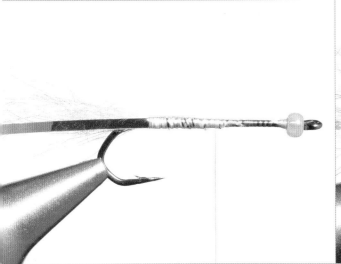 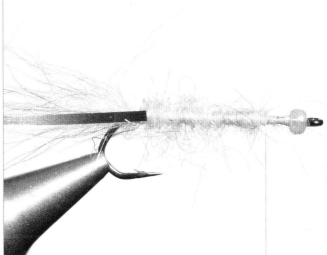

Step 1

Slide the bead up to the eye of the hook, secure with thread, then wind thread half-way along the hook shank. Tie in the tail, and then the Mylar.

Step 2

Dub SLF onto waxed thread and dub a scruffy body.

continued >

Step 3

Wind the mylar, using tight turns to trap the SLF, and tie off. Tie off the Mylar, fold it over the tie-off point and tie off again. Whip-finish, and trim.

Step 4

Using a piece of Velcro, tease out the SLF fibres. Tie in the red thread behind the hook eye, and build it up to form a neat head. Whip-finish, and apply a drop of head cement to secure.

Bob's Banger

This popper is another creation by the prolific fly-tyer Bob Popovics, with simplicity the key. It's easy to tie and durable, and the heads are easy to replace. There's nothing quite like waking up fish by having a popper bloop across the water's surface, and seeing the resultant strike. It's never subtle and always heart-stopping as the fish materialises from the depths and smashes your fly.

Poppers come in all shapes and sizes, but they all do much the same thing: their primary job is to float on or in the water's surface and push as much water as possible when retrieved (this is what triggers a response from the fish, which home in on the source of noise and vibration in the belief that it's an injured baitfish and an easy meal). As easy meals aren't always easy to come by, it's not uncommon for several fish to shoulder each other out of the way in pursuit of your offering.

Materials

Hook	Mustad S74S SS or Tiemco 811S, sizes 1–3/0	Tail	Bucktail; Gliss 'n Glow
Thread	Flat waxed nylon	Body	Estaz chenille
Head	Tiewell Soft Pops foam cylinder body; adhesive-backed prism tape	Eyes	Stick-on silver prismatic

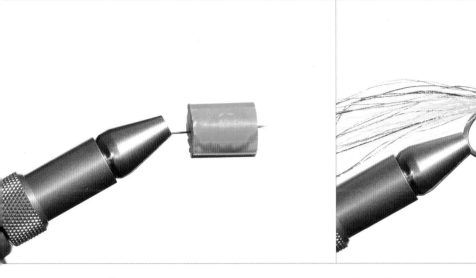

Step 1

Apply the tape to the foam cylinder with an overlap of at least 10 mm. Cut the foam in half if needed (this will depend on the hook size).

Step 2

Mark the length of the head on the hook shank. Lay a base of thread beyond this and tie in the bucktail and Gliss 'n Glow.

continued >

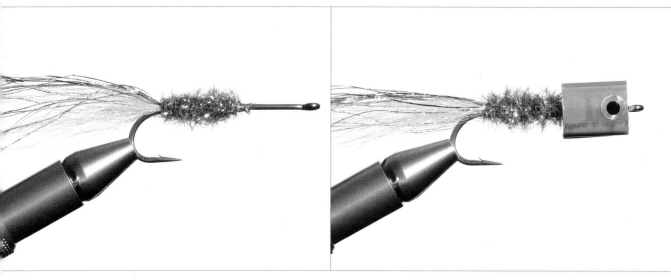

Step 3

Tie in the chenille and wrap it forward with tight turns, leaving enough space for the head. Tie off, and apply head cement to the thread.

Step 4

Apply the eyes to the body, using a smear of epoxy. Slide the head onto the hook.

CDC Emerger

Another effective emerger pattern, the beauty of this fly lies in the simplicity of its materials. CDC (or *cul de canard*) is the fluffy feathers near a duck's preen gland and contains enough natural oils to suspend the fly in the surface film. In order to keep the fly suspended, it's best to keep the body dubbing to a minimum and avoid any extra weight such as ribbing. Conversely, too long a tail will result in the fly floating rather than being suspended. If the fly is sitting too heavily in the water, try a dab of floatant on the thorax, being careful to avoid the CDC feathers.

As its name suggests, this pattern imitates a developing insect, which at this stage of its life spends a considerable amount of time hanging in the film struggling to emerge in its adult form. Fish this fly on its own and let it bob along in the current as though it's trying to sprout those wings and take off on its next adventure.

Materials

Hook	Kamasan B401, sizes 12–16	Body	Possum dubbing
Thread	Brown 6/0	Thorax	Olive dubbing
Tail	Brown cock hackle	Wing case	Natural CDC

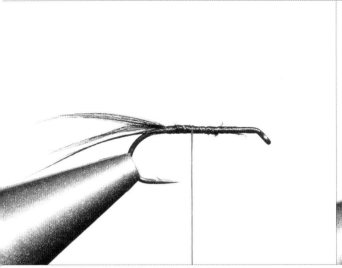

Step 1

For the tail, select four or five hackle fibres and tie them in above the hook barb. The tail should be about three-quarters the length of the hook.

Step 2

Dub a fine body to a point about halfway along the hook. Tie in the CDC at this point.

continued >

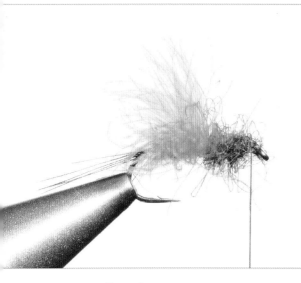

Step 3

Now dub the thorax, keeping the CDC pushed back and out of the way. Tie off the dubbing just short of the hook eye, allowing room for a small head to be formed later.

Step 4

Fold the CDC forwards to the end of the body to create the wing case. Make sure the CDC isn't pulled tight but instead forms a small loop, creating a space between it and the dubbing. Tie off the CDC and form a small head.

CIS (Christmas Island Special)

Noted American fly-tyer Randall Kaufmann began tying nearly 50 years ago and sold the flies for use in the streams of the Rockies, later developing a retail business. Fishing took him to destinations outside the US and his love of flats fishing grew. Along the way he created a number of world-class flies, including the Christmas Island Special (CIS), and as travel there has increased this fly has become a must-have pattern.

The CIS is best kept sparse – this is what makes it stand out – and, as with so many flats flies, flash is also kept to a minimum. Orange has proved to be a popular colour and a good starting point. Bead-chain eyes are perfect for shallow water and in keeping with the principles of this fly, but heavier eyes will be needed for deeper water. Cast in front of a feeding baitfish, twitch slightly if it's gone unnoticed, and hang on.

Materials

Hook	Mustad S71SSS or C68SSS, sizes 4–8	Body	Krystal Flash of same colour as the tail
Thread	Orange 3/0; flat waxed nylon	Eyes	Bead chain
		Wing	Krystal Flash
Tail	Krystal Flash	Overwing	Craft fur

Step 1

First tie in the tail. Then tie in the Krystal Flash for the body and continue the thread along the hook shank to form a base for the body. Tie in the eyes.

Step 2

Wrap the Krystal Flash up to and over the eyes, and tie off.

continued >

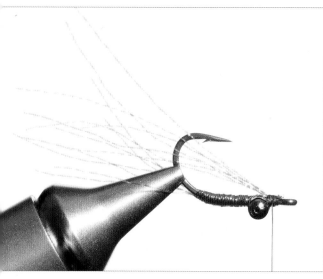 

Step 3

For the wings, invert the hook in the vice and tie in three or four strands of Krystal Flash. (You can pull the flash around to the inside of the hook and tie it in position, rather than cutting and retying.)

Step 4

Tie in a sparse overwing of craft fur. Form a neat head, whip-finish, and add a drop of head cement.

Cicada

If you are wandering along a river in New Zealand and can't hear the sound of trout rising for the racket being made in the foliage, tie on a cicada and join in! These ungainly terrestrials hatch in summertime, usually during the hottest part of the day, and more often than not end up in the drink.

There are too many variations of this pattern to list here, and really it's a fairly subjective choice. As long as it resembles the shape and colour of the living version, you're halfway there – all that remains is to put one under the nose of your quarry. In New Zealand there have been some lifelike patterns created, using spun deer-hair bodies. The pattern shown here is a simple alternative, using a foam cylinder for the body, which simply needs cutting to shape.

Materials

Hook	Tiemco 2488, size 10	Wings	Tiewell Cicada Wings
Thread	Flat waxed nylon 3/0	Legs	Rubber legs
Body	Tiewell foam		

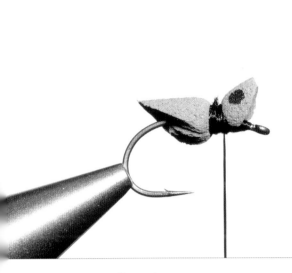 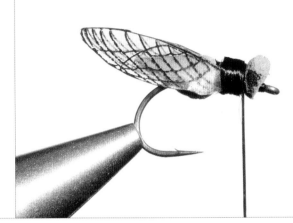

Step 1

Cut the foam body to shape and make a slit in the underside so it will fit over the hook shank. Add eyes, using a black permanent marker. Apply a few drops of super glue to the hook, fit the body and then tie in.

Step 2

Cut the wings to shape as per the manufacturer's instructions and tie them onto the body at the point where the body was tied on. A drop of super glue on this area will reinforce the fly.

continued >

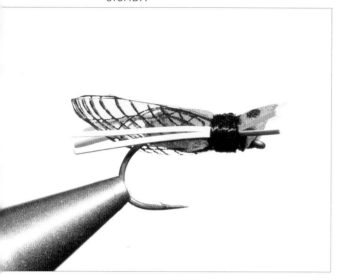

Step 3

Cut four rubber legs to the same length as the wings, and tie two per side. Whip-finish, and add a drop of head cement.

Clouser Minnow

The Clouser Minnow is one of the most successful and popular fly patterns for saltwater fishing. It was created in 1984 by Bob Clouser after Wapsi (a major US supplier of fly-tying materials) sent him their first dumbbell eyes for testing, and it's the eyes that makes this pattern so special. Tying the eyes on the back of the hook and towards its eye enables the hook to swim 'point up' and to swim with a jigging action when retrieved – perfectly mimicking the erratic movement of a baitfish and proving irresistible to fish the world over.

The wings may also be tied on the back of the hook, as originally designed, though these days they are often tied on the inside, as shown here. The White Clouser is considered *the* fly for fishing in the Weipa region of Australia's Cape York Peninsula, and will catch any fish in the tropics; it is just as effective in southern climes and can be tied in white with overwings of chartreuse, olive, grey or pink (to name but a few). Use this fly for anything with fins.

Materials

Hook	Gamakatsu SL12S or Mustad C70SD, sizes 2–4/0
Thread	Flat waxed nylon (colour to suit)
Eyes	Dumbbell, sized to suit the hook

Wing	White bucktail
Flash	Pearl Krystal Flash
Overwing	Bucktail (colour to suit)

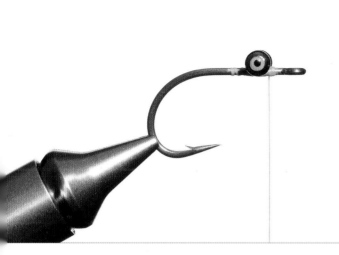

Step 1

Lay a base of thread for the eyes and tie them on the back of the hook using figure-of-eight wraps. Whip-finish, and apply a drop of head cement to secure.

Step 2

For the wings, invert the hook in the vice. Tie in a bunch of white bucktail above and in front of the eyes.

continued >

Step 3

Now tie in three lengths of Krystal Flash, doubled over and tied in at the halfway point so that you have three strands on each side of the hook.

Step 4

Tie in the overwing (here chartreuse) over and just in front of the other wing. Finally, form a neat head from the thread, whip-finish, and apply head cement. Trim the flash material to the same length as the bucktail.

Crazy Charlie

Bob Nauheim, an American angler, created this fly in the 1970s while he was fishing the Bahamas for bonefish. The fly was a success and has become one of a handful of flies that are found in every fly box on the flats from the Bahamas to Christmas Island.

Typical of bonefish flies, it's designed to be fished on the bottom, and is best tied light (i.e. sparsely dressed wings, and eyes as light as possible), which also makes for a more subtle presentation to wary fish. Colours are generally white, pink or tan, and it's best if they match the colour of the bottom. Designed with shrimp-feeding bonefish in mind, this pattern will also catch bottom-feeding species such as flathead and whiting. If you are heading to Christmas Island, tie the fly in a variety of sizes and colours.

Materials

Hook	Mustad C68SSS, sizes 4–8	Eyes	Bead chain or dumbbell
Thread	Pink flat waxed nylon	Wing	Craft fur
Body	V-Rib over silver tinsel	Overwing	Krystal Flash

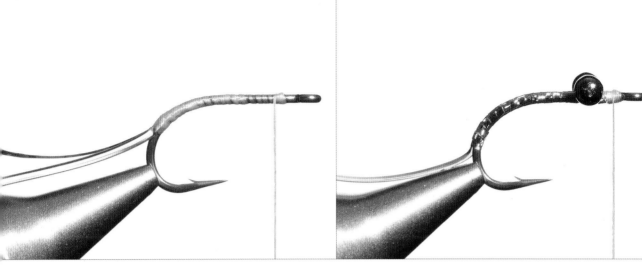

Step 1

Tie in tinsel and V-Rib at the hook bend. Pare down the end of the V-Rib before tying in, so that it sits flat on the hook shank. Continue the thread to the hook eye.

Step 2

Tie in the eyes. Wrap the tinsel up to the eyes, and tie off.

continued >

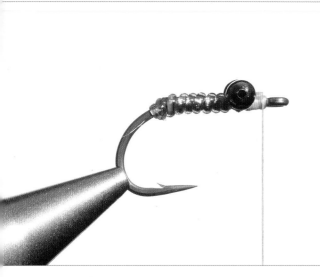

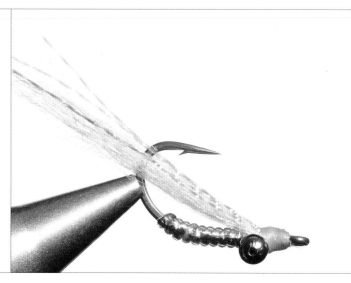

Step 3

Wrap the V-Rib over the tinsel and tie off at the eyes.

Step 4

Tie in a small bunch of craft fur and top with a few strands of Krystal Flash. Whip-finish, and apply head cement.

Crease Fly

This pattern is one of the more recent additions to the fly-fishing scene. It was created by Captain Joe Blados of Greenport on Long Island in New York, for fishing his local waters, where he guides anglers chasing striped bass and bluefish. As news of the fly's success spread, so too did the list of species that it had accounted for. Today Crease Flies are used all over the world.

As the fly bloops its way across the surface, its ability to induce surface strikes by fish such as trevally and tuna makes for exciting fishing. Colour is not as important as 'being there', but customising it is as simple as using different-coloured marker pens.

If you cast over a reef or fish-holding structure and pause between aggressive single strips, this will move more water and broadcast the fly's position.

Materials

Hook	Mustad popper, sizes 1/0–3/0	Tail	Polar Flash
Thread	Flat waxed nylon	Eyes	Stick-on
Body	Adhesive-backed foam		

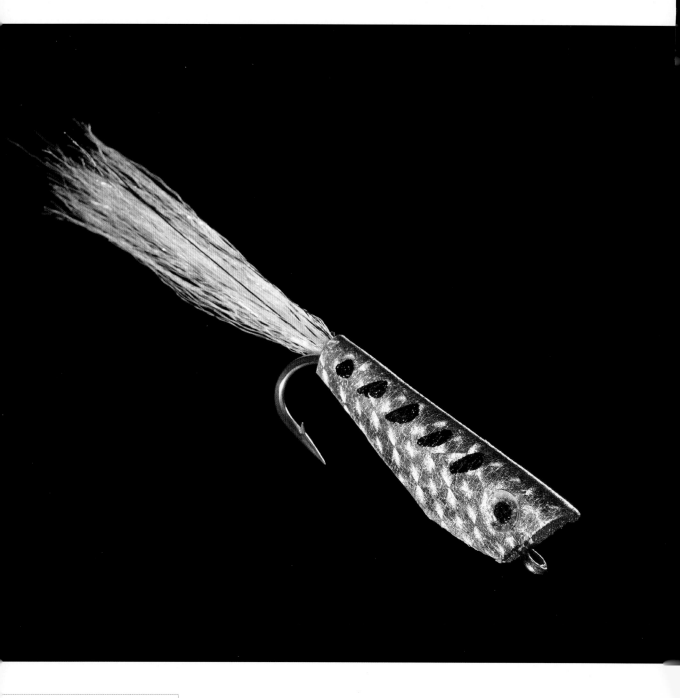

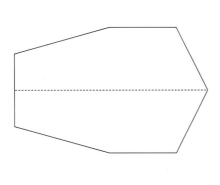

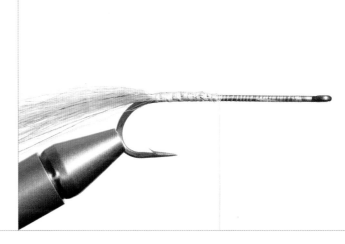

Step 1

You'll need to play around with shapes and sizes to make a template for the foam body. Cutters and templates are available, but creating your own template is as simple as cutting out a paper or cardboard shape. The finished body should have a front edge that finishes roughly perpendicular to the hook shank.

Step 2

Tie in the thread behind the hook eye and continue wrapping to the rear of the hook. Tie in a bunch of Polar Flash as a tail.

continued >

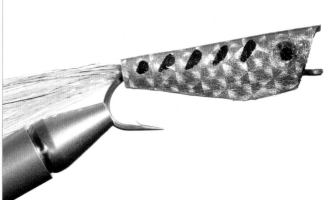

Step 3

Mix a small amount of five-minute epoxy glue – enough to coat the hook shank and the lower section of the inside of the foam. Coat both these surfaces and leave until they become tacky. Now apply one edge of the foam to one side of the hook shank (be careful when aligning the surfaces, as they may stick immediately). Fold the foam over and repeat on the other side of the hook. Hold the parts together for a few minutes, or use a bulldog clip if you are doing a few. At this stage you can also cut a teardrop shaped piece of foam and glue it into the opening at the front of the body.

Step 4

Now stick on the eyes – using five-minute epoxy glue over and under the eye will increase the durability of the fly. Finally, apply markings to the back of the fly using permanent markers: try black for stripes along the back, and red for the gills and the teardrop shape.

Dahlberg Diver

American angler Larry Dahlberg turned fly tying on its ear in the 1970s when he created this pattern, which brought together the two basic styles of flies – sinking and floating. The Dahlberg Diver utilises the natural buoyancy of deer hair to float the trimmed fly, while the shape of the fly causes it to swim under the surface.

Tied in various sizes this pattern is effective on many species of fish, ranging from Murray cod to saratoga (spotted baramundi). Cast into likely areas such as snags or lily-pads late in the day, and vary the retrieve to bring out the best in the fly: pauses in the retrieve will allow the fly to refloat itself and subsequently bloop its way through the surface, while too quick a retrieve will cause it to swim beneath the surface. If casting amongst snags, keep the fly in the zone as long as possible. Weedguards can be used, to prevent the hook getting entangled in weeds, etc.

Materials

Hook	Gamakatsu SL12S, sizes 1–4/0	Body	Black and orange deer hair
Thread	Black flat waxed nylon	Eyes	Silver 3-D
Tail	Grizzly hackle (dyed orange); black saddle hackle; pearl Krystal Flash		

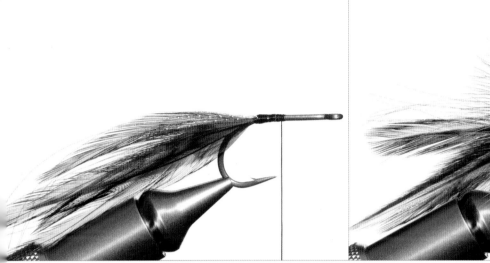

Step 1

For the tail, select matching hackles for each side and tie in so that they flare outwards. Tie in six strands of Krystal Flash between each pair of hackles.

Step 2

Select a bunch of deer hair, align the tips in a stacker and tie in as a collar over the butt ends of the hackles (do not allow the hair to spin).

continued >

Step 3

Now spin a bunch of orange deer hair, and then a bunch of black. As each bunch is spun, push it up against the preceding one to form a densely packed body.

Step 4

Repeat step 3, alternating colours, until you reach the hook eye. Using sharp scissors or a blade, trim the hair to shape (it should be flat and parallel to the hook on the underside, while the top half should be convex). Leave the rear section of the body longer. Finally, add the eyes.

Damsel Nymph

An important food item for trout, damselfly nymphs are commonly found in weed-bed margins, though structures such as sunken timber are also likely to provide habitat for them.

The choice of materials for this fly is important, but ultimately simple. Marabou is ideal for producing a slender tail with a wiggling action when retrieved, closely mimicking the strong-swimming real-life nymph. Colours are also important, with olive-green a popular choice and a good starting point. This fly can be used as a searching pattern, but be prepared to 'polaroid' feeding fish and present your fly in advance of the fish's path. Retrieves can vary from short to longer, slower strips.

Materials

Hook	Kamasan B175, size 12	Body	Olive dubbing
Thread	Olive-green 6/0	Legs	Olive hackle fibres
Eyes	Black monofilament	Wing case	Flashabou
Tail	Olive marabou		

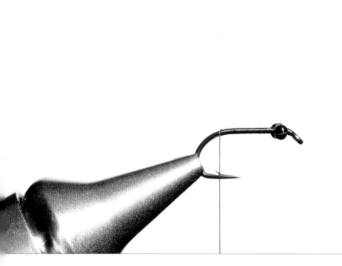

Step 1

Tie in the eyes just behind the hook eye and then run the thread back to the bend, making sure the hook is well wrapped in thread.

Step 2

Tie in the tail, which should be about one and a half times the length of the hook. Trim the marabou butts at a point just behind the hook barb.

continued >

Step 3

Begin dubbing a body, stopping about two-thirds of the way back from the hook eye. Tie in the Flashabou for the wing case at this point, then lift it out of the way and continue dubbing until you reach the eyes.

Step 4

For the legs, prepare some olive hackle fibres and tie them in behind the eyes and underneath the hook, so they are angled back slightly. Continue dubbing over the eyes and then tie off.

Step 5

Pull the wing case forward, and between the eyes, to the thread. Tie off, using a whip-finish. Trim the wing case to shape if necessary.

Del's Merkin

Del Brown's creation, the Merkin Crab, is considered one of the world's most successful permit patterns. And as Del managed to catch hundreds of these wary fish, it makes him one of world's most successful permit fishermen.

Crabs are found on all tidal flats and it's little wonder that this fly has been so effective. The clever use of yarn for the body means that tying patterns to suit the local crab colours is simple and produces a fly that is attractive to all flats species. Try mixing yarn colours to achieve a greenish hue, and make sure the weighted eyes will sink the fly quickly.

Fish come onto the flats to feed and it is important to cast in front of them, allowing enough time for the fly to sink so that it is on the bottom when the fish sees it for the first time. A short twitch of the fly, if you think it has gone unnoticed, is usually enough to spark interest and a take.

Materials

Hook	Gamakatsu SL12S, sizes 1/0–2/0	Body	Cream and tan yarn
Thread	Tan flat waxed nylon	Eyes	Dumbbell
Tail	Marabou feathers; grizzly hackle	Legs	Round rubber legs

Step 1

Tie in the thread behind the hook eye and wrap down to the bend. Tie in a small bunch of marabou and then top with two grizzly hackles.

Step 2

For the body, cut three pieces of each coloured yarn, about 40 mm long. Tie in a piece of tan yarn against the tail's tie-in point and continue along the hook shank, alternating the colours as you go. Tie in each piece using the cross-over method, (the number of layers will be determined by the hook size and the material used), keeping the yarn roughly square off the hook. Be sure to leave enough space to tie in the eyes.

Step 3

Tie in the eyes, whip-finish, and apply head cement.

Step 4

Trim the yarn to an oval shape using sharp scissors, and tie in the legs on the back of the hook using an overhand knot. The legs can be left 'au naturel', or the tips coloured red with a permanent marker.

Elk-hair Caddis

A popular fly the world over, the Elk-hair Caddis was created in the 1950s by Pennsylvanian fly-tyer Al Troth. Australian fly fishermen know only too well how effectively this pattern imitates the adult stage of the caddis fly. As dusk falls on the Goulburn River in Victoria, for example, and these flies take to the air in numbers like a whirl of snowflakes (they are known locally as snowflake caddis), the smart angler is already fishing a caddis emerger below an Elk-hair Caddis dry. This is a good two-way bet until the trout are obviously taking from the surface: the elk-hair wing makes for a buoyant fly which in a tandem rig is a good indicator for the fly below, and the white elk hair remains reasonably visible in fading light.

If the caddis are hatching, you'll be pitting your pattern against large numbers of the real fly, and you may have to cast repeatedly to rising fish before it's taken.

Materials

Hook	Kamasan B401 or Tiemco TMC 100, sizes 12–18	Hackle	Furnace
		Body	Olive dubbing
Thread	Olive 6/0	Wing	Elk hair
Rib	Fine copper wire		

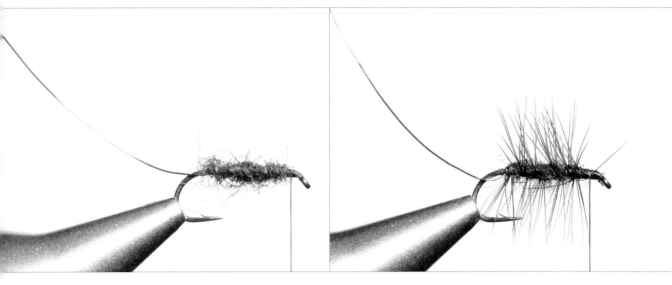

Step 1

Start by laying a base of thread along the hook, starting from behind the hook eye and finishing at a point above the barb. Tie in a short piece of copper wire. Pinch a small amount of dubbing onto the thread and form a body, gradually increasing the girth as you wind forward. Tie off, removing any excess dubbing from the thread.

Step 2

Prepare the hackle by removing fibres from the base to leave a short section of bare stem. Tie in the hackle just back from the hook eye and then palmer it evenly to the rear.

Step 3

Maintaining the tension on the hackle, wind the copper wire twice around the hook shank to secure it. Then continue winding evenly between the layers of hackle, and tie off once you reach the thread (this will hold the hackle in place). Trim off any excess wire.

Step 4

For the wings, select a small bunch of elk hair and align it using a hair stacker. Tie the hair against the end of the dubbing, make sure the hair doesn't spin but instead flares upwards against the body. Tie off, then trim the forward section of the hair at a 45° angle to the hook shank.

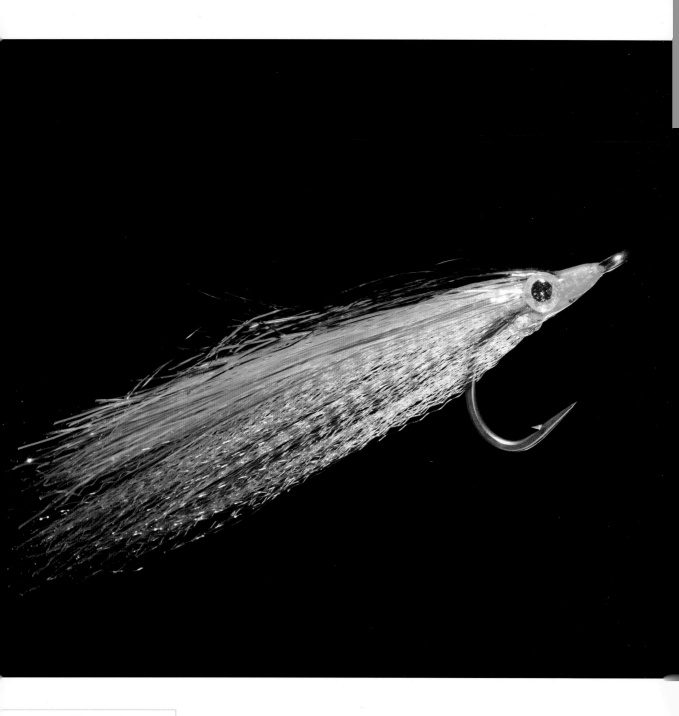

Flashy Profile Fly

The Flashy Profile Fly (FPF) is the brainchild of Australian Dean Butler and US fly-tyers Kate and Bill Howe. Dean is a game-fishing guide of world renown, responsible for a number of International Game Fish Association records, and a pioneer of taking billfish on fly. Kate and Bill designed the Anchovy Looking Fly (ALF).

The FPF has become de rigueur when in pursuit of game fish with fly tackle, though the pattern can also be tied in much smaller sizes to suit fish such as Spanish mackerel and giant trevally. As the name suggests, it's all about the profile, with everything tied on the top of the hook and nothing on the sides: this produces a slim but high-profile fly which makes casting the larger versions a little easier. These can be used to tease up fish behind a game boat; or, if your budget doesn't stretch that far, take some to Christmas Island and throw them at the resident giant trevally.

Materials

Hook	Gamakatsu SL12S, sizes 2/0–10/0	Body	Pearl Flashabou
Thread	Chartreuse flat waxed nylon	Wing	Chartreuse Super Hair
Tail	White streamer hair	Overwing	Green Flashabou

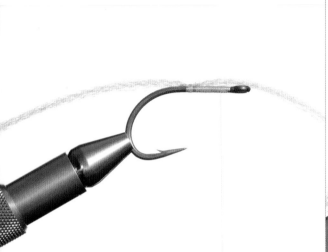

Step 1

Select a bunch of streamer hair and taper the edges by rolling the bunch between your fingers. Tie in the hair halfway along the hank and slightly forward of the midpoint of the hook.

Step 2

Fold the hank over on itself so both ends are at the rear of the hook. This is how all materials are to be tied in this pattern.

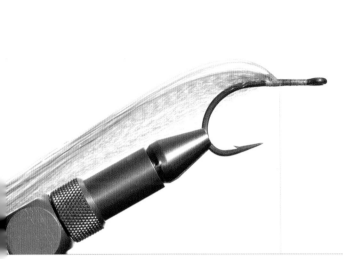

Step 3

Cut a bunch of Flashabou and taper the ends. Tie in in front of the streamer hair, fold back and tie off.

Step 4

Repeat step 3, twice more. Then invert the hook and tie in a thin bunch of streamer hair as a belly.

continued >

Step 5

Return the hook to its normal position. Tie in a bunch of chartreuse Super Hair and fold back. Top with a bunch of green Flashabou, fold back and tie off. Form a neat head with the thread, attach the eyes and coat these and the head section with five-minute epoxy glue.

Geehi Beetle

The Geehi Beetle was first tied by Dr Keith Zwar, presumably to fish the Geehi River and other waterways of the Monaro district in the Snowy Mountains of New South Wales. A warm-weather pattern, the Geehi Beetle will serve you well in sizes 12–16 and can also double as a hopper pattern if you find yourself up a river without one.

The pattern is heavily hackled, which keeps the fly afloat, and the ever-reliable peacock herl adds to the attraction. It's a fine choice for most rivers. Cast it along edges with overhanging grass, to simulate the beetles that have fallen into the river, or use as a searching pattern that's capable of convincing trout it's the real thing.

Materials

Hook	Tiemco TMC100 or 102Y, sizes 12–16	Rib	Fine gold wire
Thread	Olive	Body	Peacock herl
Tail	Golden pheasant tippets	Hackle	Furnace

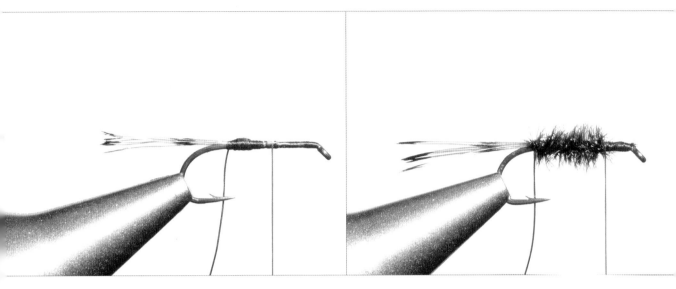

Step 1

Tie in thread behind the hook eye and lay a base of thread along the hook. Tie in the pheasant tippets as a tail (the tips should be aligned, and about the same length as the hook). Tie in a small length of gold wire.

Step 2

Tie in two pieces of peacock herl, then take the thread to a point about one-third of the way back from the hook eye. Wind each piece of herl individually to the thread, and tie off.

continued >

Step 3

Tie in a furnace hackle, wind it to the wire and secure using two wraps of the wire. Now wind the wire forward, working it between the hackle fibres so as not to crush them. Tie off once you reach the thread, and snip off any excess wire.

Step 4

Select another hackle, with fibres about one and a half times as long as the hook gape, and tie in. Wind the hackle forward, stopping just behind the hook eye, then tie off and form a small head.

Gold Bomber

The hard-bodied lure of the same name was the inspiration for Australian 'Top End' guide Mick Winterton, who created this fly after great success catching barramundi with the original.

Imitative of baitfish such as mullet, the lure's colours (gold body, black back) are paramount to the effectiveness of the fly. Other important elements are the amount of flash in the materials and the inclusion of a rattle. These can be varied, depending on the waters being fished: the dirtier the water, the greater the need for flash, vibration and bulk.

Cast this fly to fish-holding structures and leave it in the zone for as long as possible, using short sharp strips. The unweighted fly will hover in the zone more than a weighted one does, and it may be necessary to pepper an area to provoke a strike. The Gold Bomber also makes a great fly for sight-casting to barramundi and threadfin salmon when they are cruising the flats.

Materials

Hook	Gamakatsu SL12S, size 4/0 (bendback style)	Body	Gold and black Sparkle Flash
Thread	Black flat waxed nylon	Belly	Grey streamer hair
Underbody	Gold tinsel; black streamer hair	Eyes	Dumbbell; stick-on
Rattle	Glass or plastic rattle; Heat Shrink tubing		

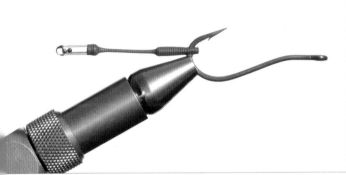 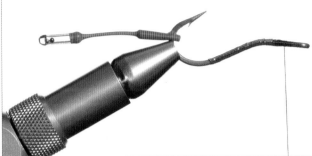

Step 1

Using a pair of pliers, bend the hook shank as shown. Insert the rattle into a piece of Heat Shrink and apply heat to shrink it onto the rattle.

Step 2

For the underbelly, tie in a length of gold tinsel and use it to wrap the hook shank.

continued >

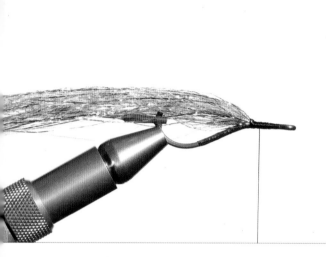
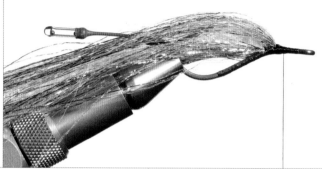

Step 3

Select a bunch of gold Sparkle Flash, tease out the ends, and tie in halfway along the shank. Fold over and tie off,

Step 4

Tie in a belly of grey streamer hair, folded over and tied in the same way as the Sparkle Flash. Then repeat step 3.

Step 5

Top with a bunch of black Sparkle Flash and tie off. Tie in dumbbell eyes and add the stick-on eyes, then tie off and coat with head cement.

Greenwell's Glory

The story starts with Canon William Greenwell returning from a day's fishing in the 1850s, with only a dun on which the elusive trout had been feeding. 'Tie some flies to match this, my good man,' he may have said. The following day Canon Greenwell was kept busy as a good number of trout fell for the soon-to-be-named Greenwell's Glory.

As with most good flies, variations evolved and today's pattern is fished as a dry, using a furnace hackle tail. Body colours can be changed to suit local insect hatches and modern threads provide an excellent array of colours, although the silk thread suggested here gives a delicacy to the body.

This is a classic fly that has stood the test of time and is still a good choice when duns are on the menu; it is a dry fly that deserves to be fished alone.

Materials

Hook	Tiemco TMC 100, sizes 14–16	Tail	Furnace hackle
		Rib	Gold wire
Thread	Pearsall's Gossamer (colour to suit) or waxed thread 6/0	Body	Pearsall's Gossamer or waxed thread
Wing	Grey duck quill	Hackle	Furnace

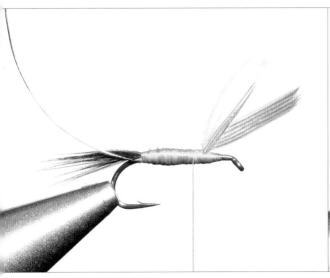 

Step 1

Begin by tying in the thread behind the hook eye. Next select two matching slips of duck quill and tie them in. Tie in the tail so that it extends about one hook length. Begin building the body by layering the thread.

Step 2

Continue builing the body, to a point two-thirds of the way along the shank towards the eye. Rib with the gold wire and then tie off.

Step 3

Tie in the hackle behind the wing, leaving the thread forward of the quills. Wind the hackle twice behind the quills and twice in front of them. Tie off, and form a small head. Whip-finish and add a drop of head cement.

Gummy Minnow

Is it a fly? Is it a soft plastic lure? Well, it's cast with a fly rod, so we'll give it the benefit of the doubt.

It all started when US fishing guide and fly-tyer Blane Chocklett set out to produce foil-backed foam, to avoid hand-laminating as some tyers were doing for Crease Flies. One thing led to another: Blane created Sili Skin and soon the Gummy Minnow was born; demand outstripped supply and now both are produced commercially.

Sili Skin is available in small sheets and a variety of colours, allowing the angler to 'match the hatch' and to tie flies in a range of sizes. This fly is perfect for throwing at skittish tuna when they are feeding on micro-bait, or for casting into a school of feeding salmon and using a flat-out retrieve.

Materials

Hook	Gamakatsu SL12S or SS15 or Mustad C70SD, sizes 2–2/0	Back	Olive Sili Skin or Crystal Skin
Thread	White flat waxed nylon	Eyes	Prismatic stick-on
Weight	Lead wire	Body	Mother-of-pearl Sili Skin or Crystal Skin
Belly	Metallic silver Sili Skin or Crystal Skin		

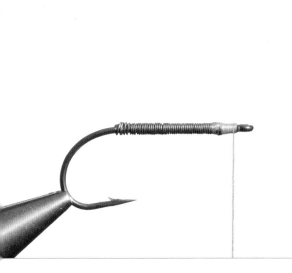

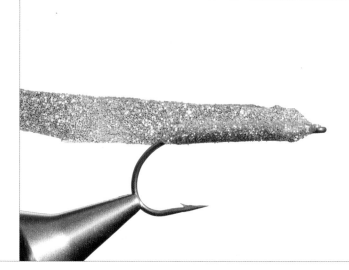

Step 1

Wrap the hook shank with thread and tie in the lead wire at the rear of the hook. Return the thread to the front of the hook, then wrap the shank with the lead wire and tie off. Cut off the tying thread.

Step 2

For the belly, cut a piece of the silver Sili Skin about twice the length of the hook and about 15 mm wide. Cut a slit in the skin so it can pass over the hook, behind the bend, once folded. Peel the backing paper off the Sili Skin and fold the skin around the hook from underneath so that it runs along the bottom of the hook shank. Trim as shown.

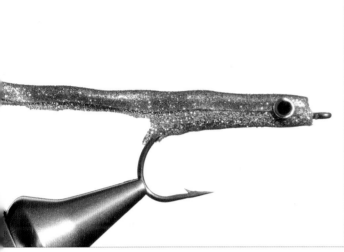 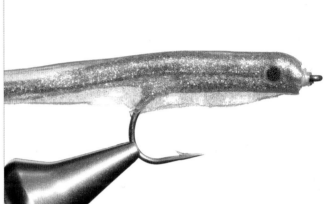

Step 3

For the back, cut a piece of olive Sili Skin about 5 mm wide and 5 mm longer than the belly piece, and stick it on top. Add the eyes. Trim the belly piece from the tail to the bend of the hook.

Step 4

Cut a piece of mother-of-pearl Sili Skin large enough to comfortably cover the fly. Place it on the back of the hook and fold down. Press together, ensuring all edges are sealed. Reattach the thread and tie off the front of the Sili Skin body. Trim the outer layer to the required shape.

Gurgler

Innovative American fly-tyer and author Jack Gartside brought us the Gartside Gurgler around 20 years ago. Popular with US striped-bass fisherman, the fly is also increasingly used in Australia. Neither a popper nor a slider, the Gurgler picks up on the benefits of both and rolls them into one. Shortening the body length enhances the action, as the rear section of the fly will sit lower in the water and be dragged through the surface.

These variations make it an ideal pattern for barramundi or bass where casts are made over lily-pads or weed-beds and the fly is skipped back, often taken on the pause in retrieves. Bass fishermen will find this fly perfect when surface strikes are the order of the day.

Materials

Hook	Gamakatsu SL12S or Mustad C68SS, sizes 2–3/0	Belly	Chenille
Thread	Flat waxed nylon	Body	Yellow closed-cell foam
Tail	Chartreuse bucktail; Krystal Flash	Gills	Red Krystal Flash

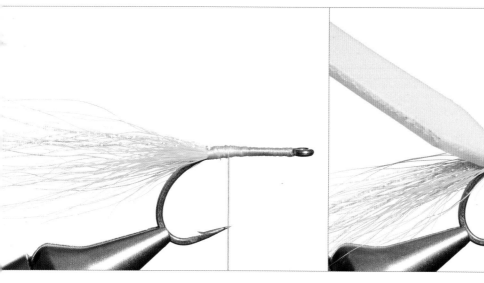

Step 1

Run the thread along the hook shank and tie in both the tail materials.

Step 2

Cut a strip of foam about 10 mm wide for a size 1/0 hook. Shape the end of the foam before tying in (it should be tapered, so that it squashes down against the hook when wrapped with thread). Lay the foam on the hook and tie off above the barb.

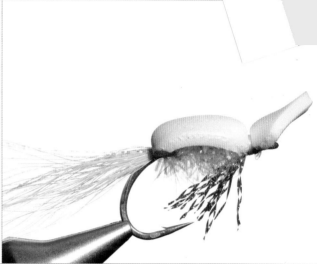

Step 3

Tie in the chenille at the tie-in point of the foam. Advance the thread to about one eye's length back from the hook eye. Wrap the hook shank with chenille, and tie off.

Step 4

Bring the foam forward over the chenille, and tie off. Invert the hook and tie in a few strands of the red Krystal Flash. Trim the head section of the foam to shape.

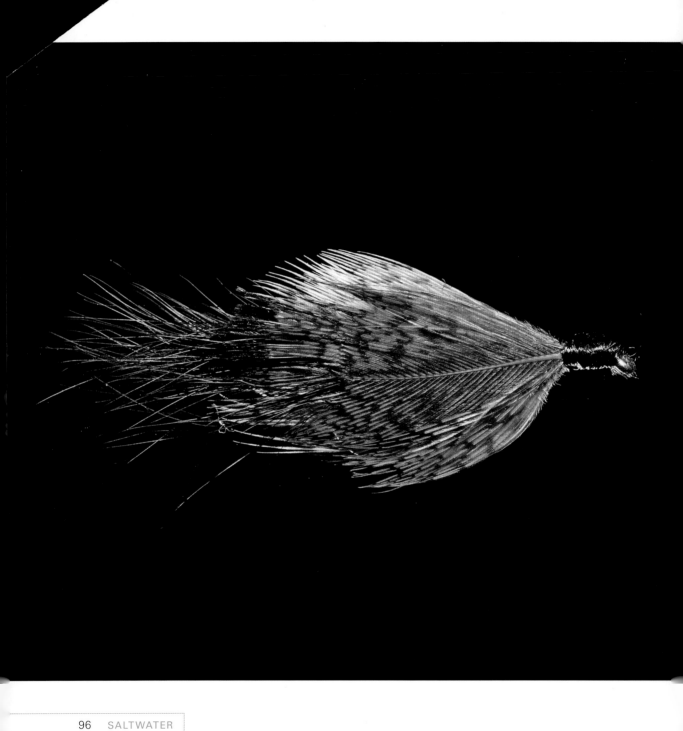

Hamill's Killer

It was during the 1960s that New Zealander Bill Hamill adapted the original 'killer' fly to better match what the trout of Rotorua were feeding on: he substituted dyed olive partridge as the wing material, and tied pheasant tippets over the tail. Success was immediate, news of the pattern spread, and this is now a popular wet fly on both sides of the Tasman. Today's versions include weighted bodies using fine lead wire under a body of chenille or wool.

Hamill's Killer remains a proven fish-taker and is a good choice for lakes as a general searching pattern. It's worth having weighted and unweighted versions, and experimenting with the retrieve. Don't be afraid to use the odd quick strip, to let the fish know Hamill's is about.

Materials

Hook	Kamasan B830 or Tiemco, sizes 6–10	Body	Yellow or red wool, or chenille
Thread	Black 6/0	Wing	Olive-dyed partridge
Tail	Black squirrel tail; golden pheasant tippets		

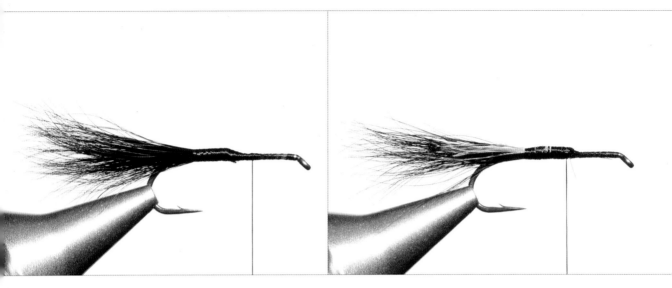

Step 1

Select a bunch of squirrel tail and tie in, extending it beyond the hook by about a hook length.

Step 2

Over this, tie in the pheasant tippets. Use a partridge feather as a guide: the tippets should project just beyond the length of the feather.

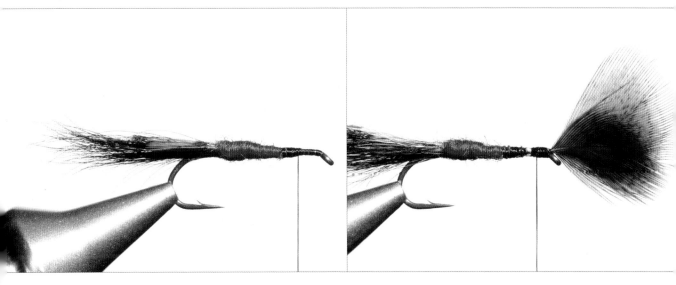

Step 3

Tie in wool at the base of the tippets and take the thread to the front of the hook. Wind the wool forward to the thread, and tie off.

Step 4

Select two partridge feathers of equal size and lay them on the fly to gauge the position and size required. Once these are decided, strip some fibres off the stems of the feathers and tie in, making sure the feathers are aligned. Trim the butts, and add a drop of head cement.

continued >

Step 5

If required, align the feathers by pulling on the quill butts. Now fold back both pairs of feathers, and tie off. Make sure the feathers are aligned before you form a head with the tying thread. Coat the head with varnish.

Hare and Copper Nymph

The Hare and Copper Nymph has proved to be one of the most successful nymph patterns for waters on both sides of the Tasman. It doesn't exactly represent a particular nymph – it's more of a general pattern – but it has been the undoing of many a trout. Are the fish trying to tell us something?

The body is formed from hare's-ear fur; the rougher the effect, the better. For good measure in bigger waters, add weight by wrapping lead wire along the hook shank, building up where the thorax will be formed, and tie in a bead head. Fish the weighted version on its own when the fish are holding deep; the unweighted version is suitable for use in a tandem rig.

Materials

Hook	Kamasan B175 or Tiemco 9300, sizes 10–16	Rib	Copper wire
		Body	Hare's ear dubbing
Thread	Brown 6/0	Weight	Lead wire (optional: see introduction above)
Tail	Pheasant tail fibres		

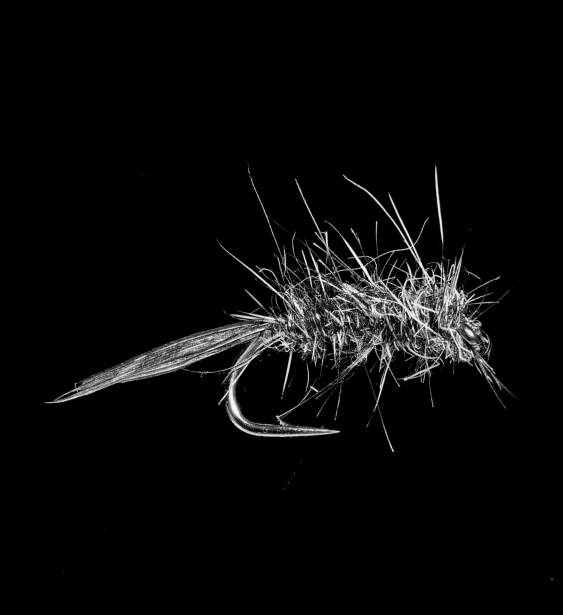

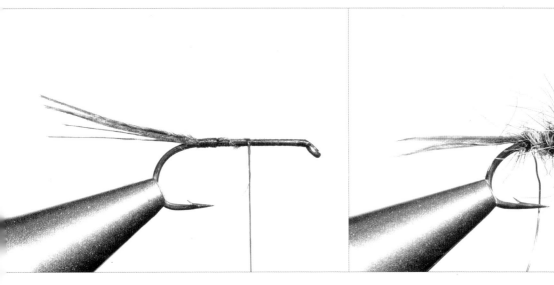

Step 1

Tie in thread behind the hook eye and wrap the hook with thread down to the bend. Tie in the tail.

Step 2

Tie in the copper wire and then dub a tapered body using the hare's ear fur. The aim is to produce a bulky, scruffy body.

continued >

Step 3

Wind the copper wire evenly to the hook eye and tie off. Using a dubbing needle, pick out the longer guard hairs in the dubbing, to suggest legs.

Hopper

Not too much science here. It's hot, there's a slither in the grass on your left, you scare a grasshopper into flight and it lands in the river. Trout eats grasshopper. You've already tied on a hopper pattern that matches the size and colouration of the creature you just helped along to its untimely demise, and now you know where your quarry is. Crouching low to the water, all you need is a short cast to present the imitation and another hopper goes down the hatch.

Hopper patterns are like chocolate-cake recipes – there are hundreds, and most of them work. Whichever one you decide on, it must be light and buoyant, and preferably be tied with legs. Foam bodies are a godsend for this style of pattern, keeping the fly afloat and visible to the angler. Australian fly-tyer Muz Wilson's Wee Creek Hopper, shown here, is a lesson in simplicity: it floats all day and remains intact despite trout finding it a tasty morsel.

Materials

Hook	Tiemco TMC 100, sizes 10–14	Wings	Elk hair
Thread	Yellow 6/0 or 3/0	Legs	Orange round rubber legs
Body	Tiewell's Ezyhoppers foam body		

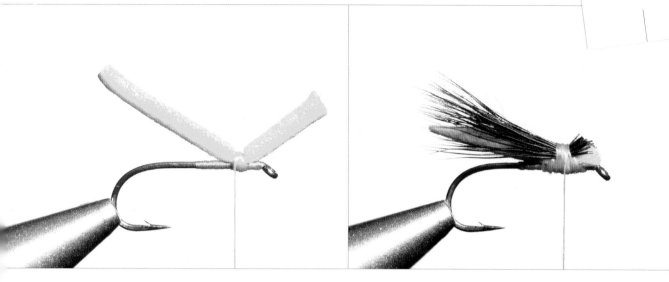

Step 1

Cut foam to about one and a half times the length of the hook. Attach the thread to the hook where the body will be tied in, and add a drop or two of super glue. Tie the body in firmly, so that the foam 'kicks up'.

Step 2

Trim both ends of the foam parallel to the hook. For the wings, select a small bunch of elk hair and stack it until the tips are aligned. Tie the hair in so that the wings extend just beyond the body. Trim the butts behind the front end of the foam.

continued >

Step 3

Tie in the legs. To complete the fly, work the thread under the head and then whip-finish against the hook. Trim the legs so that the front legs are shorter than the rear ones.

Keel Fly

Keel Flies have been around for some time, and this Aussie version by Ken Culgin further enhances the pattern's fish-catching qualities. Ken has used 3-mm lead solder as a keel, which is then encased in epoxy: the end result is a fly that sinks quickly but, more importantly, performs a fishy jig when retrieved.

Ken's pattern has seen action on impoundment barramundi, mackerel and tarpon, to name but a few. A different size and colour is used for each of these very different fishing situations, such is the versatility of this pattern. Retrieves will vary from one species to another, from very short for barramundi (making sure the fly stays in the zone for as long as possible) to high-speed retrieves for big queenfish in the deep.

Materials

Hook	Gamakatsu SL12S, sizes 1/0–6/0	Lateral Line	Black Gliss 'n Glow
Thread	Flat waxed nylon	Gills	Red Supreme Hair
Weight	3-mm lead solder	Overwing	Sparkle Flash
Body	White Unique Hair	Eyes	Stick-on

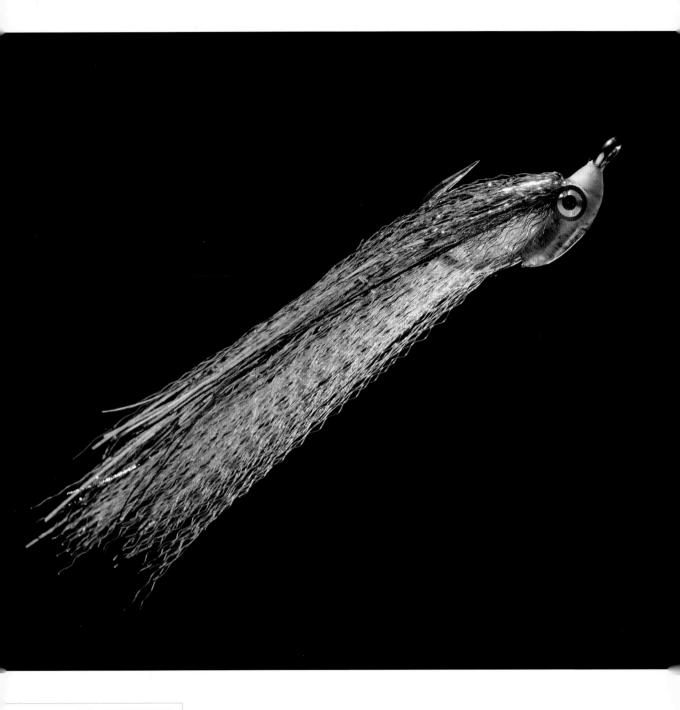

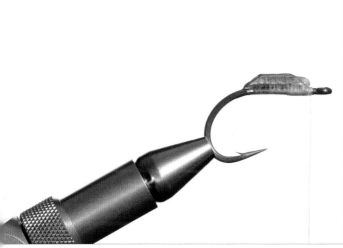

Step 1

Cut a piece of solder to shape (try to make the cuts so that the rear shoulder is longer than the front one), then bind it to the hook. (Score the solder, especially the ends, in a pair of pliers to stop the thread from slipping.) Apply a light coat of five-minute epoxy to hold everything in place.

Step 2

Invert the hook in the vice. Tie in two small bunches of white Unique Hair, followed by a few strands of Gliss 'n Glow for the lateral line.

continued >

Step 3

Next tie in a short bunch of red Supreme Hair for the gills. Tie in a few strands of Sparkle Flash for the overwing.

Step 4

Mix some five-minute epoxy and apply a light coat to the body. Apply the eyes once this coat has tacked off, and coat these also when applying a second layer of epoxy. (Ken likes to mix glitter into the epoxy, for extra effect.) Trim the fly to shape.

Klinkhammer Special

Dutch angler Hans van Klinken created this pattern in the 1980s, his aim being to produce a fly that sat as deep as possible in the surface film while still remaining visible to the angler. Enter the Klinkhammer (or Klinkhåmer), which is visible to the angler courtesy of the wing post while the abdomen, more importantly, is visible to the trout below.

This fly, which imitates an emerging nymph, can be tied to suit local hatches such as dun or caddis flies by varying colours, materials and sizes. Whichever recipe fits the bill, be sure to maintain the basic principle of this pattern – abdomen deep in the surface film, wing suspending the fly. If the fish are taking insects from the surface, try greasing all but the last few centimetres of the leader so that the fly remains suspended there; otherwise, allow the fly to sink slowly through the water column.

Materials

Hook	Kamasan B100, sizes 12–18	Hackle	Natural dun
Thread	Tan 8/0	Body	Tan dubbing
Wing Post	Hi-Vis	Thorax	Peacock herl

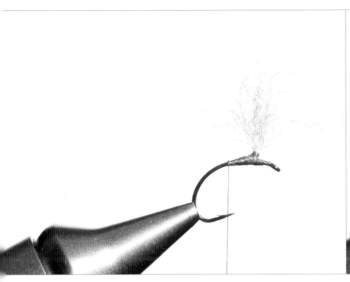

Step 1

Tie in the thread where the wing post will be located. Cut a small piece of Hi-Vis and tie in along the hook shank. Pull the Hi-Vis upright and make a number of turns in front of the post to keep it vertical, then wind the thread around the bottom of the Hi-Vis to form the base for the hackle.

Step 2

Tie in the hackle at the base of the wing post and wind the thread back along the hook. Apply a small amount of tan dubbing and form a slender body, stopping short of the post.

continued >

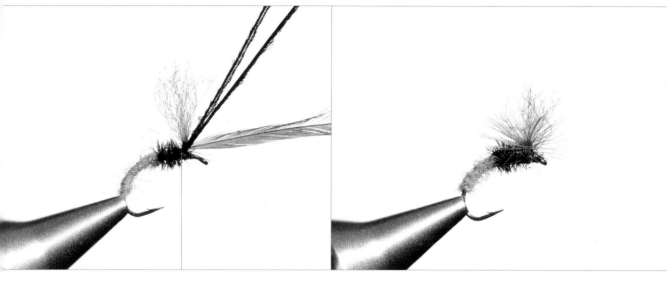

Step 3

For the thorax, tie in two pieces of peacock herl, then advance the thread to the wing post and wind the herl up to the post. Tie off at the base of the post, but don't trim yet.

Step 4

Wind the hackle downwards from the top (about four or five turns) and tie off. To complete the fly, wind the peacock herl forward and tie off.

Kosciusko Dun

The Kosciusko Dun (or Kossie Dun, as it is more fondly known) was named by the late Mike Spry, who in the 1970s ran a guiding business from the township of Khancoban in the Mt Kosciusko foothills in New South Wales. The dun fly of this region is one of Australia's largest, and Mike studied the insect for some time before creating his pattern. Luckily for us he got it right, and his pattern has accounted for many fish in rivers from the Snowy Mountains across the border into Victoria.

As the pattern can be tied on hooks as large as size 10, the body needs to be plump and the hackle full – the trout will be looking for large specimens. Fish this fly alone on a long leader when the Kossie duns are on the move.

Materials

Hook	Tiemco TMC 100 or Kamasan B401, sizes 10–14	Hackle	Buff-coloured
		Tail	Buff-coloured hackle fibres
Thread	Light brown 6/0	Body	Cream or light tan dubbing
Wing	Buff hackle tips		

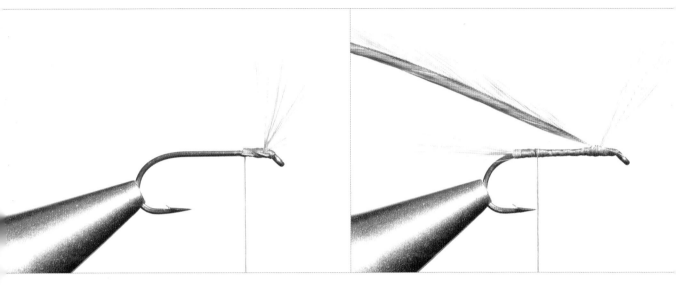

Step 1

Tie in a base of thread for the wing. Tie in the hackle tips so that they lie along the hook shank and extend over the hook eye. Once secured, stand the tips up and make a number of turns in front of the wing.

Step 2

Tie in the hackle and then take the thread to the rear of the hook. Tie in a tail roughly the same length as the hook.

continued >

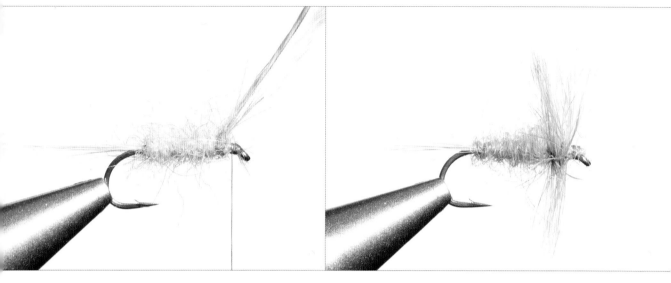

Step 3

Next, dub a body, building a nice taper as you near the hackle tie-in point. Continue the dubbing to just short of the hook eye, and tie off.

Step 4

Wind the hackle to the hook eye, and whip-finish. Apply a drop of head cement to secure.

Lefty's Deceiver

America's favourite fly-fishing identity, Bernard 'Lefty' Kreh, designed this fly for striped bass in the waters of Chesapeake Bay. It has become such a celebrated pattern in the US that a postage stamp has been created in its honour. And rightly so: it's a good generalist pattern for saltwater, mimicking baitfish and easily tied in various sizes and colours to suit local species. Importantly, it casts well courtesy of the bucktail collar, and a jerky retrieve imparts enough action to trigger a response from most predators.

All-white is a good starting point for this fly and will fool most fish, especially when used with red gills. Traditionally this pattern is tied with a topping of peacock herl, but synthetic substitutes such as bucktail or Supreme Hair will be more durable. Deceiver patterns will catch most fish in the salt, and if a clouser isn't working, tie on one of Lefty's. A good fly for Spanish mackerel when fished down a berley trail.

Materials

Hook	Gamakatsu SL12S, Mustad C70SD, sizes 1/0–4/0	Body	Silver tinsel; white bucktail
		Gills	Red Krystal Flash
Thread	White flat waxed nylon	Collar	White bucktail
Tail	Bucktail; white saddle hackles; pearl Krystal Flash	Wing	Blue bucktail

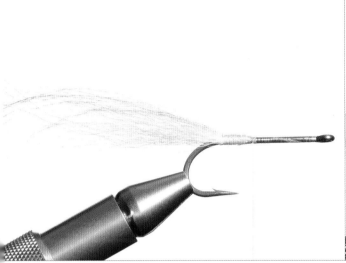

Step 1

Tie in the bucktail and Krystal Flash as a tail.

Step 2

Select three matching hackles for each side of the hook, and tie in so they are pointing inwards (make sure they are balanced, so that the hook will act as a keel and keep everything upright). Apply super glue to the tie in-area. Tie in the silver tinsel and advance the thread two-thirds of the way to the hook eye. Wrap the hook shank with the tinsel, and tie off. Tie in red Krystal Flash as gills.

continued >

Step 3

Take a bunch of white bucktail and tie in on the side of the hook. Repeat on the other side, to form a collar.

Step 4

Top with blue bucktail. Tie off, then form a head with the thread. Attach eyes and apply a thin layer of epoxy.

Matuka

The Matuka is a New Zealand pattern created in the first half of the 20th century. A grand old fly harking back to a time when trophy trout were plentiful, it is still worthy of inclusion in today's fly box. Originally it was tied with the feathers of the matuku (a native bittern), until the species became endangered (hopefully not from over-zealous fly-tyers) and their use was banned. There were plenty of substitutes available and today's versions include grizzly hackle and rabbit.

The fly is tied to imitate the local baitfish and is great on waters like Lake Taupo in the centre of the North Island, where it is used as a searching pattern. As with other wet flies, vary the retrieve once the desired depth is achieved.

Materials

Hook	Mustad 3666, sizes 2–10	Body	Yellow chenille
Thread	Red 6/0	Wing	Badger hackle
Tail	Red hackle tips	Hackle	Badger
Rib	Fine gold wire		

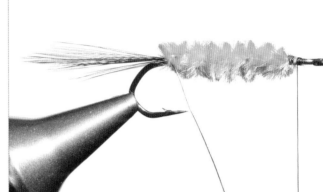

Step 1

Lay a base of thread along the hook shank. Tie in a small bunch of red hackle fibres as a tail. Then tie in the gold wire and the chenille.

Step 2

Advance the thread to the front of the hook. Wrap hook with the chenille to form the body, and tie off.

continued >

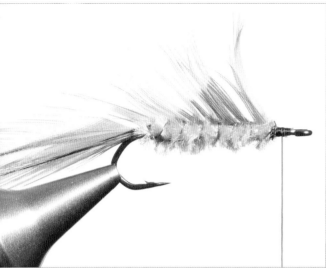

Step 3

For the wing, first prepare two matching badger hackles so they fit over the body. This is done by removing fibres equal to the length of the hook, from one side of the feathers. Tie them in at the front of the hook, then wind the gold wire forward through the hackle, ensuring no fibres are trapped, and tie off.

Step 4

Tie in the hackle and wrap three or four times, making sure that the curve of the hackle is facing you so that the fibres lean back. Form a small head, tie off and then apply a drop of head cement.

McVay's Gotcha

'Gotcha!' the angler said time and time again, as Jim McVay's pattern nailed another bonefish. The name stuck and the fly has continued to catch bonefish. It has changed a little, though, since McVay first tied it: he used tufts of carpet from a taxi for his earliest patterns, it is said, but nowadays craft fur is the preferred wing material. Bead-chain eyes are the norm for this pattern, but dumbbells may be required to increase the fly's sink rate in deeper water or stronger currents.

Essential for that trip to Christmas Island, this fly will also take local species such as flathead when fishing estuaries. Allow it to sink, and then retrieve with short strips kicking sand off the bottom.

Materials

Hook	Mustad C68S-SS, sizes 4–8	Tail	Pearl Mylar
Thread	Pink flat waxed nylon	Body	Pearl Sparkle Braid
Eyes	Bead chain or dumbbell	Wing	Tan craft fur; Krystal Flash

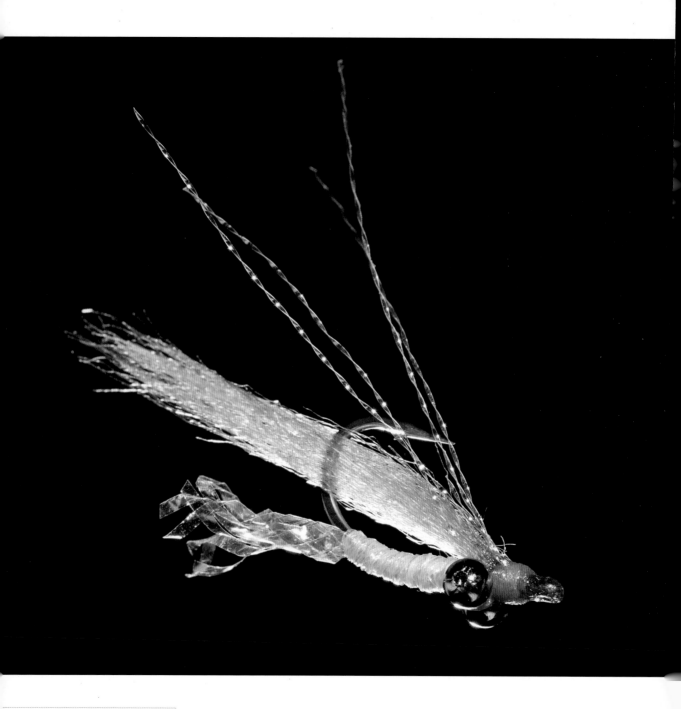

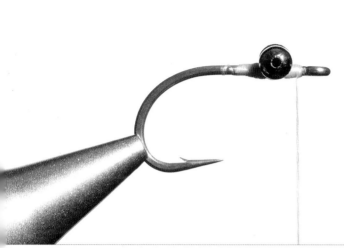

Step 1

Tie in the eyes.

Step 2

Remove the core of the Mylar and tie in the Mylar behind the eyes. Continue tying the thread to the hook bend and then cut the Mylar to length. Fray the ends.

continued >

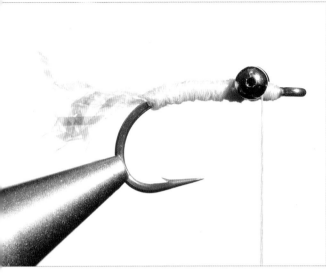

Step 3

Tie in the Sparkle Braid and advance the thread to just behind the eye of the hook. Wrap the body with the braid, continuing over the eyes, and tie off.

Step 4

Invert the hook in the vice and tie in a wing that finishes beyond the tail. Top with a few strands of Krystal Flash, tie off, and form a neat head. Apply a little head cement.

Midge Pupa

Also known as a buzzer, this pattern imitates Chironomid (midge) pupa. Found in still waters, these small insects often occur in very large numbers and are a major part of the trout's subaquatic diet. Midges are often described as a nondescript insect, and modern patterns are simple affairs that can be little more than a hook wrapped in floss or ribbing material. The inclusion of a thorax and cheeks adds life, however, and like the natural these flies need to be slender in form.

A light breeze is a boon when fishing buzzers, as the wind blowing your line will impart enough action to the fly; otherwise, a slow figure-of-eight retrieve, punctuated by lengthy pauses, can be enough to entice a strike. If fish are seen taking midges from the surface, particularly ball-like clusters of mating midges, a tandem rig using a midge-ball pattern can be employed to cover all bases.

Materials

Hook	Kamasan B100 or Tiemco 2487, sizes 12–16	Cheeks	Orange floss
		Thorax	Black dubbing; Flashabou
Thread	Black 8/0 or 6/0	Breathers	White Antron yarn
Body	Red floss; black flat waxed nylon		

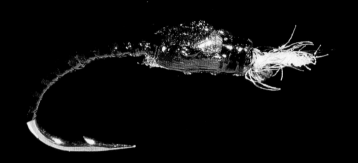

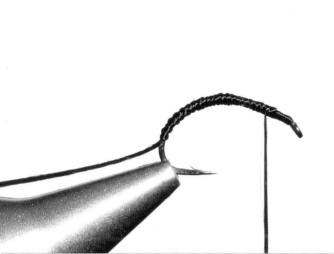

Step 1

Tie in the red floss behind the hook eye, and wrap down to the bend. Tie in a length of black thread, then wrap the floss back along the hook to the cheek tie-in point. Whip-finish with two turns, to secure.

Step 2

Now use the black thread to rib over the body, and tie off.

continued >

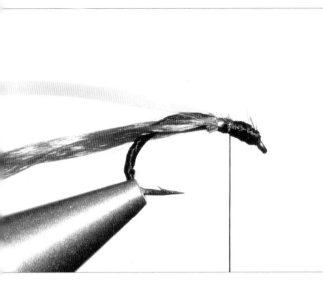

Step 3

To form the cheeks, cut two lengths of orange floss and tie in on each side of the hook; leave hanging. Tie in a short piece of Flashabou, and leave till step 4.

Step 4

Apply a small amount of black dubbing to the thread, dub a small thorax and then tie off just behind the hook eye. Tie in a tuft of white Antron, to form breathers. Now bring the cheeks forward and tie off. Pull the Flashabou forward, tie off, and form a neat head. Coat the completed fly with varnish.

Muddler Minnow

Muddler or Moedler? The latter is the name of a German migrant to the USA in the 19th century, who is known to have fished with a spun deer-hair fly. Whether or not he gave his name to the muddler we know today is anyone's guess, as is the extent to which it influenced Don Gapen when he created his Muddler Minnow pattern in the mid-20th century. It's not inconceivable that the two events are quite unrelated.

Confused? Don't be. This is a great fly to fish with at night, using a black version. Slowly retrieve with the odd jerk and pause thrown in, making sure you don't lose contact with the fly. The spun deer-hair head typically used for this pattern produces buoyancy, and when retrieved slowly the fly pushes a good amount of water which creates a wake that the trout home in on.

Materials

Hook	Tiemco 9300 or Kamasan B401, sizes 8–12	Body	Gold tinsel
		Wing	Black duck quill
Thread	Black 6/0	Collar	Black deer hair
Tail	Black deer hair	Head	Black deer hair

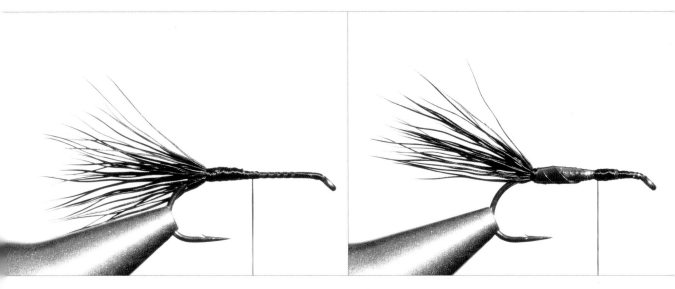

Step 1

Tie in thread behind the hook eye and continue down to the bend. Tie in a small bunch of deer hair to produce a tail that extends about three-quarters of a hook length. If the tail splays out a little, that's okay, as this will add to the wake and the buoyancy.

Step 2

For the body, tie in the tinsel and advance the thread about three-quarters of the way towards the eye. Wind the tinsel to this point, and tie off.

continued >

Step 3

Tie in a pair of black crow slips, ensuring they are of matching length.

Step 4

Tie in the deer hair for the collar: it needs to spin around the hook and flare back. Stroke the hair back to form a collar over the wings, and wrap the base with thread.

Step 5

For the head, tie in and spin small bunches
of deer hair until you reach the hook eye.
Whip-finish the thread. Trim the head to
shape, making it slightly flatter on the
lower side of the hook.

Mudeye

The mudeye is the nymphal stage of the dragonfly and, owing to its prolific numbers, an important food source for trout. The hatch and migration of mudeyes usually occurs at dusk, continuing into the evening as the nymphs climb from the water onto available landing places (such as fallen tree limbs), before starting their adult life. As darkness descends, the sounds of trout taking mudeyes from the surface signal where the action is, so cast to the sounds of a rise or, if the light allows, to the ripple left behind.

The mudeye pattern can be tied as either a dry fly or a wet, and it's worthy having both patterns in your fly box. While there are many variations using materials such as foam, spun deer hair, dubbing and fur, the pattern shown here uses chenille for its ease of forming the body. Extra weight can be achieved by using lead on the hook shank, or by selecting bead-chain eyes in lieu of monofilament.

Materials

Hook	Tiemco 9300 or Kamasan B175, sizes 8–12	Body	Chenille
		Legs	Deer hair
Thread	Black 6/0	Wing	Duck breast feathers
Eyes	Black monofilament	Head	Chenille

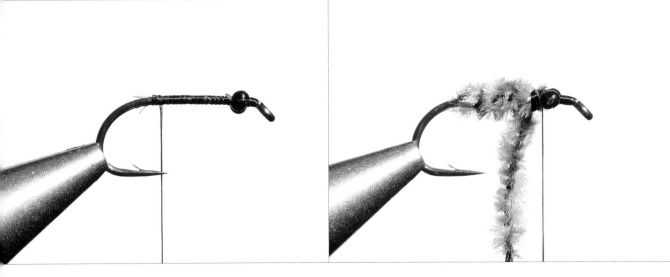

Step 1

Tie in the eyes and then run a base layer of thread, finishing at the bend of the hook

Step 2

Tie in the chenille and advance the thread to just behind the eyes. Wrap the chenille up to the thread and secure it (don't cut it yet).

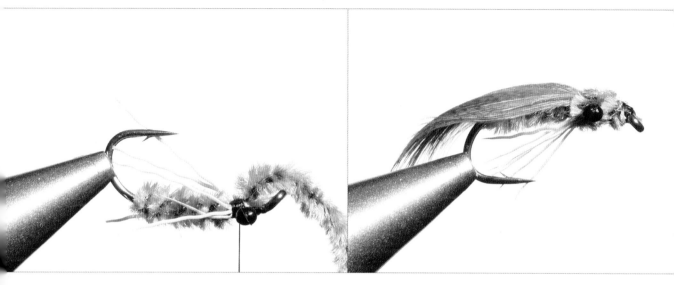

Step 3

Invert the hook and tie in a small bunch of stacked deer hair as legs. Trim the butts.

Step 4

Return the hook to its normal position and tie in the wing. Continue wrapping the chenille over the eyes to form the head, then tie off. Add a drop of head cement.

Orange Spinner

The life cycle of the mayfly provides the angler with an array of patterns and opportunities. Having left the water the mayfly emerges as an adult, ready to mate, and hovers, 'dancing' vertically to attract females. Some fish seize the opportunity and take the insects as they linger too close to the surface, but it is more likely that they will wait for easier pickings as – sapped of energy from their final fling – the insects (thence known as spinners) fall helplessly to the water, wings spreadeagled.

Fly patterns need to display the insects' wings as they are viewed from the trout's perspective: this can be achieved in various ways, a clipped hackle being a good starting point. The tail is tied from microfibbetts (you can use two or three) that are splayed to match the natural form.

Materials

Hook	Tiemco TMC 100 or Kamasan B401, sizes 12–16	Rib	Fine gold wire
		Body	Orange seal fur
Thread	Orange 6/0	Hackle	Cock furnace
Tail	2 or 3 microfibbets		

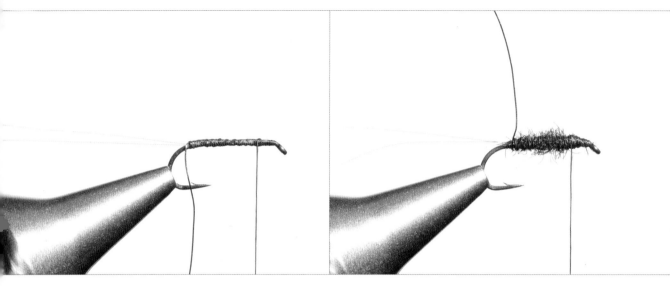

Step 1

Tie in the thread at the hook eye and continue to the bend. Tie in two microfibbetts so that they splay out slightly. Tie in a length of gold wire.

Step 2

Form a dubbing loop from the thread, apply the seal fur sparingly, and spin to form a rope. Wrap the dubbing rope to produce a slim body, and tie off.

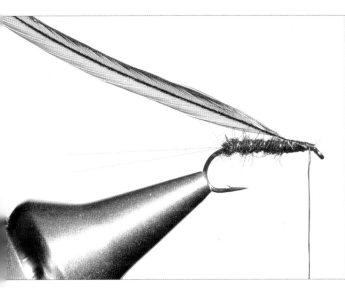

Step 3

Now wind the gold wire to the thread, then tie off and remove. Tie in a hackle, continue winding the tying thread to the hook eye, and secure.

Step 4

Wind the hackle to the hook eye, and whip-finish. The underside of the hackle can be clipped to imitate a spent spinner's wings, which can be useful later in the evening.

Parachute Adams

Following on from a pattern tied by Leonard Halladay as a spent-wing dry fly, the Parachute Adams allows the body of the fly to sit beneath the water's surface, visible to the trout and a great trigger for a response: from below, the hackles resemble the legs of an emerging dun struggling to free itself from the water.

The original was considered a good fly and many think this version even more potent. The white calf-tail wing post affords the angler improved visibility, which is so important in fading light and fast water. It's a great dry fly that catches fish anywhere, so don't leave home without a few.

Materials

Hook	Tiemco TMC 100, sizes 12–16	Hackle	Grizzly and cock furnace
Thread	Brown 6/0 or 8/0	Tail	Brown and grizzly hackle fibres
Wing	White calf tail	Body	Grey dubbing

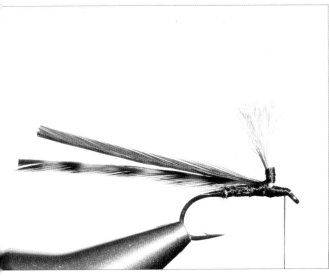 

Step 1

Start the thread behind the hook eye and form a base for the wing. Tie in a bunch of calf tail and wind the thread around and up it to form a post for the hackle. Tie in one grizzly and one furnace hackle.

Step 2

Continue the thread to the bend of the hook and tie in the tail. Dub a body, continuing to the front of the wing.

Step 3

Remove any remaining dubbing material from the thread. Wind the hackles around the post – start high and work downwards – then tie off, removing any excess. To form a head, apply another small amount of dubbing and continue to the hook eye.

Pink Thing

Created by Australian Graeme White, the Pink Thing has attained iconic status amongst fly-fisherman chasing barramundi. Like so many other great flies, it was born out of the frustration of having fish take the lure rather than the fly: Graeme set about creating a fly that resembled the successful lure, thus swinging the odds back in favour of the fly fisher.

Using the attributes of deceiver-style flies and the Given's Barred and Black as a starting point, Graeme developed the Pink Thing, enhancing it with a bulkier collar that pushes water – a key to the success of this fly. Mono weedguards, dumbbell eyes, rattles and different hackle colours can all be used to suit differing conditions. Casting among snags and drains, using short jerky retrieves to impart a jigging action to the fly, will invariably result in takes. Don't limit this fly to barramundi, though – try mottled colours for other natives such as yellowbelly and cod.

Materials

Hook	Gamakatsu SL12S, size 4/0	Wing	Grizzly hackles
Thread	White flat waxed nylon	Collar	Crosscut rabbit zonker; two pink hackles
Tail	White saddle hackles; pearl Flashabou		
Body	White bucktail; Krystal Flash	Eyes	Bead chain (or weighted, as appropriate)

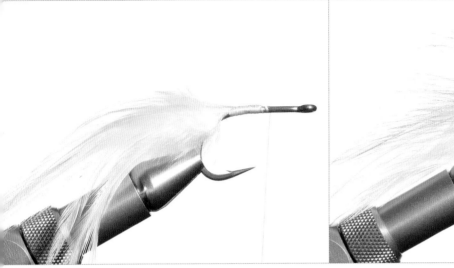 

Step 1

Tie in three white saddle hackles on either side of the hook, then tie in the Flashabou.

Step 2

Tie in a bunch of bucktail to form a collar over the hackle butts. Tie a second collar in front of the first.

Step 3

Add three strands of Krystal Flash along each side of the hook. Now tie in two grizzly hackles per side, to form the wing.

Step 4

Tie in a length of rabbit zonker in such a way that the hair falls back naturally when the strip is wound around the hook.

continued >

Step 5

Wrap the rabbit zonker, using three turns, and tie off. Now tie in the pink hackles and palmer these forward in tight turns to produce a collar. Tie off the hackles, making sure you leave enough room for the eyes. Tie in the eyes, form a neat head with the thread, and tie off (against the hackles) behind the eyes.

Polar Fibre Minnow

Designed by South African Paul van Reenen, the Polar Fibre Minnow is (much like a deceiver) more of a tying style than a pattern, allowing the angler to create a fly to match the hatch.

The semi-translucent Polar Fibre is naturally tapered along its length, which means the fly holds its shape in the water and at the same time its body pulses with every strip of the retrieve. Although the Polar Fibre was originally tied in this baitfish pattern, its success has seen it used in Surf Candies and Clousers. The minnow version is tied in a high-tie style, making for a slender-bodied fly with a fishy profile – a great fly for pelagics. Try pink-backed flies and cast into tuna schools boiling on the surface, and strip hard.

Materials

Hook	Mustad C705D, or Gamakatsu SL12S sizes 2–2/0	Lateral Line	Silver Gliss 'n Glow
		Gills	Pink Fluoro Fibre
Thread	Flat waxed nylon	Eyes	Silver self-adhesive
Body	White and pink Polar Fibre		

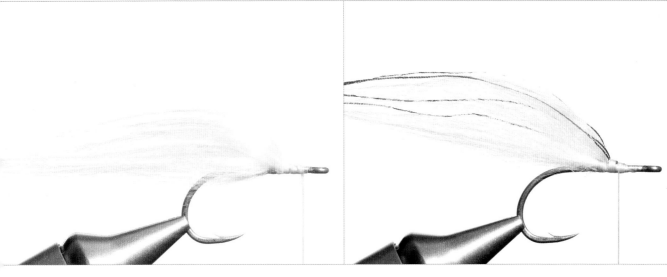

Step 1

Run the thread along the hook shank. Tie in a bunch of white Polar Fibre, catching only a millimetre or two of the material. Tie in a second bunch.

Step 2

On top of the white Polar Fibre, tie in two or three strands of Gliss 'n Glow on each side of the hook, as a lateral line.

continued >

Step 3

Tie in the first layer of pink Polar Fibre.

Step 4

Tie in a second layer of pink Polar Fibre, then use a comb to blend the layers to form the minnow profile. Invert the hook and tie in a short bunch of pink Fluoro Fibre as the gills. Add eyes and coat with five-minute epoxy, using just enough to cover the eyes and form a small head section.

Red Tag

Look in most fly boxes and you're bound to find some Red Tags. It started life in the mid-19th century as a wet fly, but soon evolved into a dry. Since its introduction to Australian waters, it has successfully caught trout in places as far apart as mainland alpine streams and Tasmanian lakes, and in most rivers in between.

There is no doubt the Red Tag resembles a beetle in shape, although it's generally considered to be a non-imitative fly and can work at any time. Given the popularity of this fly, it's little wonder that there are many variations on offer, and it certainly lends itself to a little experimenting at the vice. Bodies can be plump and full, tied from peacock herl or deer hair, and hackles can be oversized. A great little fly for 'putting the feelers out'.

Materials

Hook	Tiemco 100 or 102Y, sizes 10–16	Tail	Red wool
		Body	Peacock herl
Thread	Black 6/0	Hackle	Furnace

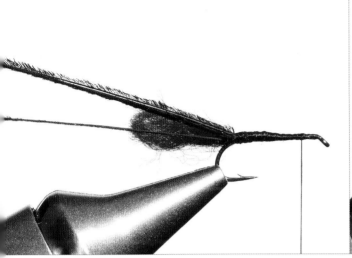

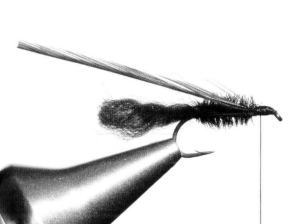

Step 1

Start the thread behind the hook eye and wind down to a point just behind the barb. Tie in a small amount of red wool and leave long (it will be trimmed later). Now tie in three strands of peacock herl and advance the thread two-thirds of the way towards the hook eye.

Step 2

Wind one strand of herl along the hook as far as the thread, and tie off. Repeat this step with the next two strands of herl, being careful not to pull too tight or to crush the preceding herl. Once you have a satisfactory, gently tapered body, tie in the hackle.

continued >

Step 3

Wind the hackle four or five times, tie off and form a neat head behind the eye. Treat with a small drop of head cement before trimming the red wool.

Rob Laspina's Permit Fly

Rob Laspina operates as a guide at Hinchinbrook Island on the central Queensland coast, and he has a good idea of what will fool a fish. Although designed with the holy grail of flats fishing – the permit – in mind, and as a specialised version of other prawn patterns, his permit fly has also become a favourite of anglers fishing the flats for the likes of golden trevally and blue bastards.

Unlike many other prawn patterns, this one rides point-up (as do all good flats flies) and is tied on the reverse side of the hook. Balance is important in a pattern like this, and the over-use of epoxy and body materials can cause the fly to tip over: keeping everything to a minimum will ensure that the hook gape remains open and clear for solid hook-ups, and that the fly rides upright. Cast ahead of feeding fish, allowing the fly to sink and rest on the bottom before twitching slightly to catch their attention.

Materials

Hook	Gamakatsu SL12S, sizes 1–2/0	Feelers	Krystal Flash
		Legs	Krystal Flash
Thread	Flat waxed nylon	Eyes	30 lb monofilament
Body	Tan Super Hair	Antennae	Krystal Flash

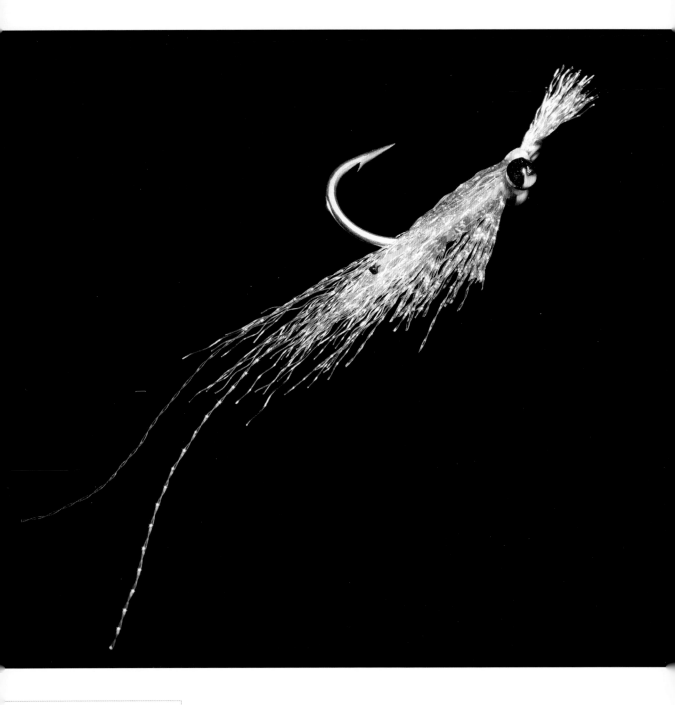

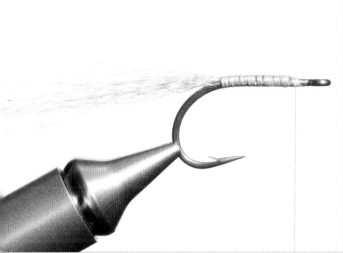 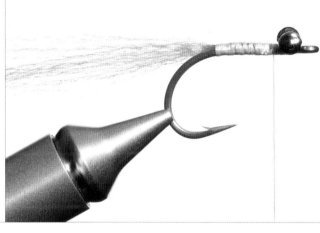

Step 1

Tie in a bunch of Super Hair (leave it long, to be trimmed later).

Step 2

Tie in the dumbbell eyes.

continued >

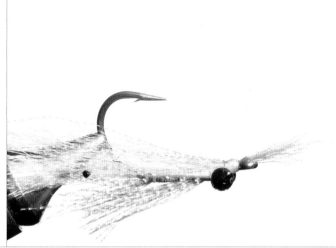

Step 3

Cut a couple of pieces of monofilament and burn the ends to create blob-like eyeballs. Colour these black with a permanent marker, tie one on each side of the hook and then trim off any excess. Tie in a couple of bunches of Krystal Flash on the bottom of the hook, for feelers.

Step 4

Invert the hook, tie in another bunch of Super Hair and top with two long strands of the Krystal Flash as antennae.

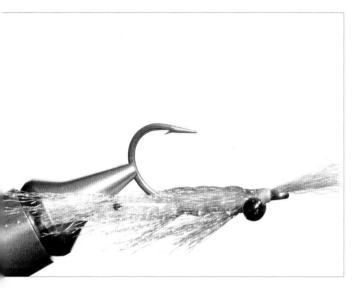

Step 5

Apply a light coat of epoxy and work it into the material, ensuring that the hook gape is kept as open as possible. Now trim the Super Hair to shape (the idea is to create a mouth by forming a V between the two layers of hair).

Royal Humpy

Jack Dennis created this variation of the Yellow Humpy (which was devised specifically for the fast-flowing streams of the Rocky Mountains), preferring to use elk hair rather than deer hair due to its toughness and the additional flotation provided by its hollow form. The result is a buoyant attractor pattern that is at home on fast rough water. Is it a beetle? Is it a hopper? Who cares, it works.

The Royal Humpy is a heavily hackled fly – perfect for added flotation, but also likely to pass the scrutiny of trout as it bounces along. On a good day this pattern is capable of enticing trout from the cooler depths, and it's always a good fly to have in the box on hot summer days when the terrestrials are in their sights. Like many other general dry patterns, it works well when used in a tandem rig in deeper flows.

Materials

Hook	Tiemco TMC 100, sizes 10–16	Tail	Dark-brown deer hair
		Overbody	Elk hair
Thread	Black 6/0	Body	Red floss
Wing	Calf tail	Hackle	Furnace

Step 1

Tie in the thread at the hook eye. Then tie in a bunch of calf tail about one-third of the way back from there (tie the wing so that it is upright and divided). Tie in some deer hair, making sure the tips are level, then trim off any excess.

Step 2

Select a bunch of elk hair and align the tips using a hair stacker. Remove the tips and tie in the elk hair behind the wing. Continue wrapping back to the hook bend.

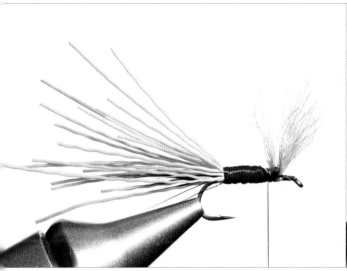

Step 3

Tie in the red floss and take the thread back to the wing. Wrap the floss to form a plump body, and tie off behind the wing.

Step 4

Bring the elk hair over the body and tie off at the wing, taking care that the hair has a uniform shape. Tie in a furnace hackle.

continued >

Step 5

Wind the hackle twice behind the wing and two or three times in front of it, then tie off.

Royal Wulff

For more than 50 years, Lee Wulff was a pioneer and innovator in fly fishing in America. The Royal Wulff is a legacy of his dry flies of the 1920s, evolving in response to a need for greater robustness. The introduction of deer hair for the tail and calf tail for the wings not only provides strength, but also acts as an attractor in rough water.

This heavily dressed pattern is best fished in fast water, where it will float high and, courtesy of the divided wing, remain highly visible to the angler as it races along with the current. It won't go unnoticed by trout lurking in deeper sections, either, and they'll rise to take it. While not representing any creature in particular, this fly can work where hoppers or beetles are present and is a good early-season choice, either fished alone or as the dry in a tandem rig.

Materials

Hook	Tiemco TMC 100 or Kamasan B401, sizes 12–16	Tail	Deer hair
		Body	Peacock herl; red floss
Thread	Black 6/0	Hackle	Brown or ginger cock
Wing	White calf tail		

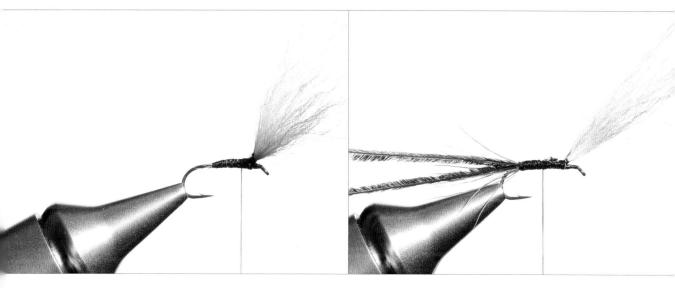

Step 1

Tie in the thread back from the hook eye and form a small base onto which the wing will be tied. Tie in a bunch of white calf tail so that the tips extend beyond the hook eye, removing any excess from the butt ends. Pull up the calf tail and use fig-ure-of-eight wraps to divide it and so form two wings.

Step 2

Stack a small bunch of deer hair and then tie it in to produce a tail that extends about a hook length past the bend. Secure the hair by wrapping the thread along both the hair and the hook shank. Tie in two strands of peacock herl and advance the thread about one-third of the way towards the wing.

continued >

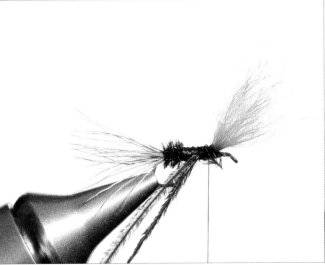

Step 3

Wrap the herl to the thread, and tie off. Now tie in a short piece of red floss at the point where the peacock herl is tied off. Wrap the floss so that it's a little longer than the section of herl, then tie off. Then tie in two more pieces of herl and advance the thread to just short of the wing.

Step 4

Wrap the herl until you reach the thread, then tie off. Tie in a hackle and wind this three or four turns behind the wing and two turns in front of it. Tie off, form a small head, and whip-finish.

Squid Fly

Everything eats squid, from snapper and kingfish over inshore reefs to yellowfin tuna in the blue water, as a result of which there are nearly as many squid patterns as there are squid. Fly-tyers such as Bob Popovics have designed a number of patterns, which have no doubt inspired other tyers, and the pattern shown here is a general one.

While there is a vast array of Squid Fly styles, they should always have prominent eyes and move fluidly when retrieved. The tentacles of the squid also need to exhibit some liveliness underwater, and there are a few options to consider – rubber legs, legs cut from the skirt of a game lure, and white saddle hackles, to name but a few. The methods, style and materials for a squid pattern are really only limited by your imagination. Cast over reef areas and retrieve with short jerky strips and long pauses.

Materials

Hook	Mustad S74SS or Tiemco 811S sizes 1/0–3/0	Tentacles	White saddle hackles; Flashabou
Thread	White flat waxed nylon	Body	Estaz chenille; E-Z Body Braid
Weight	Lead wire	Eyes	Prismatic

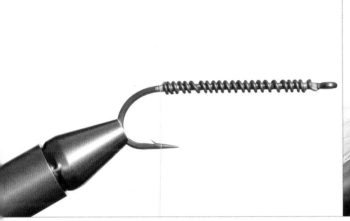

Step 1

Lay a base of thread and tie in the lead wire. Wrap the hook shank with the wire, and tie off.

Step 2

Tie in six slender white hackles and a few strands of Flashabou above the end of the hook. Apply five-minute epoxy at this point and along the lead wire.

continued >

Step 3

Tie in the chenille and wrap to the hook eye, using tight turns. Cut a piece of braid, slide over the hook eye, and tie off.

Step 4

Push the braid back over itself and the chenille, down to the bend in the hook. Tease the ends out a little and stick on the eyes. Apply a small amount of five-minute epoxy under and over the eyes.

Squimp

Originally designed by Texan Cary Marcus as a bonefish fly for the flats of Belize in central America, the Squimp has gained popularity as a general flats fly. Borrowing all the triggers of prawn and crab flies, the Squimp combines the legs typical of crab patterns with a prawn-style body – a bit of an each-way bet. Foraging fish doubtless find it hard to resist, as the legs provide the right amount of movement as the fly is twitched along the seabed; and with dumbbell eyes, the fly rides point-up, reducing the chance of snagging on the seabed and optimising hook-up rates.

Colours for this pattern can be easily altered, but tan and olive are popular. If polaroiding fish, cast well in front of them; if fishing 'blind', use short strips to retrieve the fly to stir up puffs of sand, and let the legs come to life during pauses.

Materials

Hook	Mustad S71SSS or Gamakatsu SS15, sizes 8–1/0	Tail	Tan craft fur; rubber legs
		Body	Tan chenille
Thread	Pink flat waxed nylon	Wing	Tan craft fur
Eyes	Spirit River I-Balz	Legs	White rubber legs

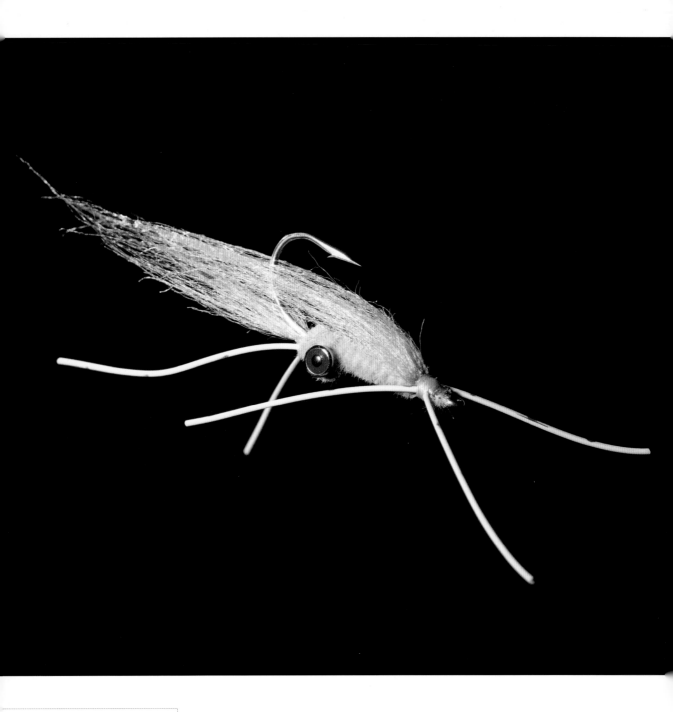

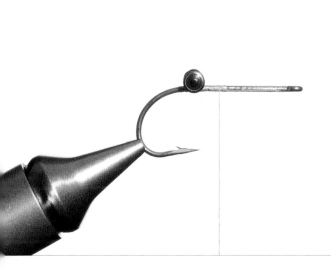

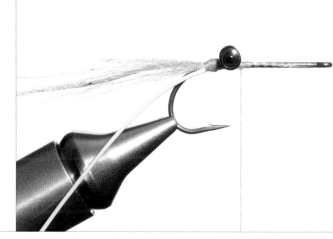

Step 1

Tie in the eyes above the point of the hook.

Step 2

For the tail, first tie in the craft fur and then tie in two rubber legs (on each side of the hook).

continued >

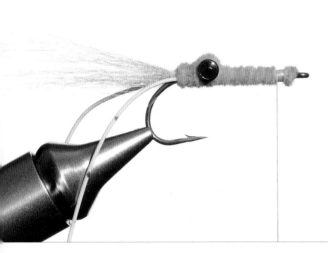

Step 3

Tie in the chenille, advance the thread to the front of the hook and wrap the chenille to this point. Tie off the chenille.

Step 4

Invert the hook in the vice and tie on the wing material at the end of the chenille. Now tie one rubber leg to each side of the hook so that they both splay out in an X shape. Whip-finish, and add a drop of head cement. Colour the legs with a permanent marker for extra effect.

Stick Caddis

The Stick Caddis represents the larval stage of the caddis fly, a soft-bodied creature which either builds its own home from grass or stick matter or takes up residence in a hollow stick or reed.

Typically a stillwater fly, this has been a consistent winner on lakes and is considered by many to be a must-have for fishing such waters. Its success has provided inspiration for fly-tyers the world over, and there are many variations to choose from. By using pieces of fly line for the stick, fishing at different depths is simply a matter of deciding whether to select the pattern tied with a floating or a sinking body. It pays to be vigilant when fishing flies like the Stick Caddis: stay connected to the fly and strike at the first hint of a take.

Materials

Hook	Kamasan B175, size 14–10	Legs	Grizzly hackle fibres
Thread	Brown 6/0	Head	Golden yellow Super Bright dubbing
Body	Fly line; chestnut Antron dubbing		

Step 1

Wrap the hook shank in thread. Cut a piece of fly line about 40 mm long, tie it to the top of the hook and then bind it to the shank. Colour the tail section of the fly line with a permanent marker to match the chestnut body dubbing.

Step 2

With the thread, form a dubbing loop at the hook bend. Apply the Antron dubbing to the loop and spin until you have a fine rope. Wrap the dubbing on the tail section of the fly line first: this can be a little difficult, but you can fill any gaps later. Before you reach the end of the line, measure where you want the 'stick' to finish and then apply a tiny smear of super glue to catch the dubbing rope and stop it slipping. Wrap the fly line back along the hook, filling in any gaps, to about two-thirds of the way towards the hook eye.

continued >

Step 3

Invert the hook and tie in a short clump of grizzly hackle for the legs. Form another dubbing loop and apply the Super Bright dubbing: again, spin the loop to form a rope and then dub the head section. Tie off, and remove any excess material. Finally, trim the fly line to leave it slightly longer than the dubbed section.

Surf Candy

The Surf Candy is the fly pattern for which its creator, Bob Popovics, is best known. Bob introduced the use of epoxy as a body in the quest for more durable flies, and further enhanced this with synthetic wing material – and so the Surf Candy was born. Today it is an essential pattern for the pursuit of fast-moving pelagics such as tuna and salmon, being easy to cast and simple enough to tie to match the hatch.

Popular colours are all-white, or white with olive, grey or blue backs. Use eyes as big as possible for the body size (depending on their size, it may help to crease them before applying). Gills can be drawn on with a permanent marker if desired, but in the hurly-burly of a bust-up, the fish won't notice. The trick is to have on hand a pattern that matches, in both colour and size, what the fish are feeding on, deliver it with a quick and accurate cast, and strip hard.

Materials

Hook	Gamakatsu SL12S, sizes 2–2/0	Wing	White and blue Super Hair
Thread	Flat waxed nylon	Lateral Line	Krystal Flash
Body	Sparkle Braid or tinsel	Eyes	Self-adhesive (see note in introduction, above)

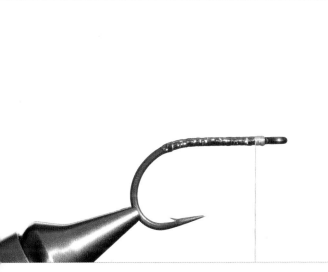

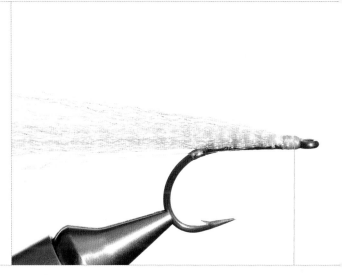

Step 1

Start the thread behind the hook eye and wrap it down the shank to the start of the bend. Tie in the braid or tinsel, and advance the thread to just behind the hook eye. Wrap the shank with the body material, and tie off.

Step 2

Select a bunch of white Super Hair and tie onto the top of the hook, allowing it to fan partially around the hook.

continued >

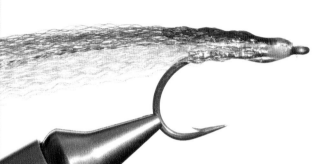

Step 3

Tie in two strands of Krystal Flash per side: to do this, cut two strands from the hank and tie them in at their halfway point. Next tie in a small bunch of blue Super Hair, and tie off.

Step 4

Mix a small amount of five-minute epoxy on a flat surface (e.g. a double thickness of aluminium foil): keep the mixture as flat as possible and avoid stirring too vigorously as this will create bubbles. Apply the epoxy as a thin coat, ensuring that you work it between the layers and under the hook shank. Before the epoxy loses its tackiness, pull everything back into line making sure the lateral lines are aligned.

Step 5

Once the first coat of epoxy has dried,
stick on the eyes. Apply a second, light
coat of epoxy and rotate the fly until
the glue begins to set, using a bodkin to thin out any blobs. Make sure the
epoxy extends to the hook bend, as this
will reduce the risk of the fly's tail wrapping. Using sharp scissors, trim the fly to
shape.

Toad Fly

This was first tied by US angler Gary Merriman in pursuit of coastal tarpon. Today's patterns sport a marabou tail in lieu of the original rabbit strip, and it's this version that has been successful in the rivers of Cape York in far northern Australia. No doubt the extra action afforded by the marabou has increased the versatility of the fly, but its profile and water-pushing capabilities make it suited to casting into thick cover and tempting the likes of barramundi into nailing it before it gets away.

The colours of flies are always the big variable, and what works today may not succeed tomorrow. Green, green and green seem to be the most effective colour for this fly, which takes bonefish as well as tarpon and barramundi. The fly works best when cast to structures and fished dead-drift, so that the motion of the water makes the materials pulsate seductively. Throw in the odd strip to create a wake, but try to keep the fly in the strike zone.

Materials

Hook	Gamakatsu SL12S or Mustad C68S-SS, sizes 1–4/0	Tail	Marabou
		Collar	Zonker strip
Thread	Chartreuse flat waxed nylon	Body	Sparkle yarn (or similar)
		Eyes	Black monofilament

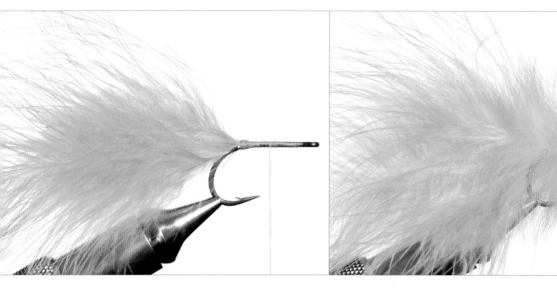

Step 1

Wrap the hook with thread and tie two marabou quills on the bend of the hook.

Step 2

Now tie in the zonker strip, palmer a dense collar (use two or three turns only), and tie off.

Step 3

Cut the yarn into short lengths (about 40 mm) and tie onto the hook shank using the crossover method.

Step 4

Add eyes, whip-finish, and apply a drop of head cement. Now trim the yarn to an oval shape, using sharp scissors.

Tom Jones

Unlike its namesake this fly may not attract underwear-throwing ladies, but it is certainly a magnet for fish. Originally tied by Australian John Lanchester in the 1970s, for use in his home waters of Victoria, the Tom Jones has become a standard in most fly collections. The beauty of the fly is its ability to represent a range of aquatic life, making it ideal as a searching pattern and, naturally, effective for casting to smelters.

Since the Tom Jones was first designed, fly-tyers have tinkered with materials, shapes and sizes, such is the versatility of this pattern and its ability to imitate various food sources. Fish it using a slow figure-of-eight retrieve punctuated with the odd short strip.

Materials

Hook	Kamasan B175, size 10	Rib	Copper wire
Thread	Black 6/0	Body	Olive dubbing
Tail	Black squirrel tail	Wing	Wallaby belly fur or zonker strip

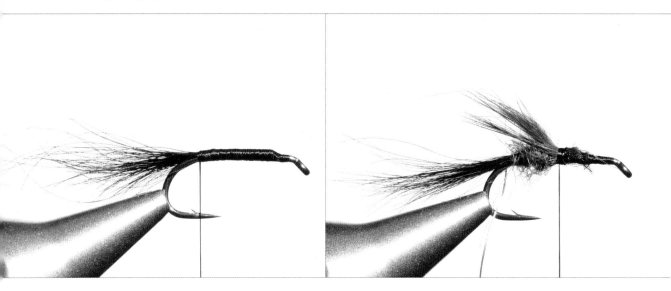

Step 1

Lay a base of thread and tie in the tail.

Step 2

Tie in a short length of copper wire. Add dubbing to the thread and dub a non-tapered body, stopping about one-third of the way along the hook shank. Tie in the first wing, using a sparse bunch of wallaby fur or zonker.

Step 3

Continue dubbing to just behind the hook eye. Tie in the second wing.

Step 4

Now wind the copper wire forward to produce an evenly ribbed body, and tie off at the head. Whip-finish and add a drop of head cement.

Ultra Shrimp

Another creation by the master of epoxy flies, Bob Popovics. Fish love to eat crustaceans and this fly will appeal to bream in southern Australian waters and barramundi in the north.

When tying this fly there are a couple of points to remember. First, depending on what size fly you are tying, form the carapace using the minimum amount of material and also use minimal epoxy, as too much of either will tend to tip the fly and it will swim upside down. Second, don't extend the epoxy too far beyond the hook bend, as this may reduce hook-up rates. Cast to fish-holding areas such as wharf pylons, estuaries, and mangroves, and use a slow retrieve with occasional short, sharp strips.

Materials

Hook	Gamakatsu SL12S or Mustad C70S-D, sizes 2–2/0	Tail	Tan Super Hair
		Legs	Orange-dyed grizzly hackle
Thread	Tan or pink flat waxed nylon	Eyes	20 lb monofilament
Body	Tan Super Hair	Carapace	Five-minute epoxy

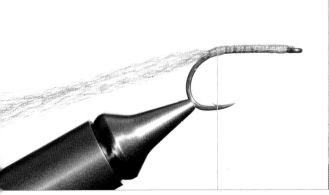

Step 1

Lay a base of thread along the shank and tie in a sparse bunch of Super Hair on the top of the hook. Wrap the thread along the length of the hair and pull down as you reach the end so that the hair tips point downwards.

Step 2

Tie in a shorter bunch of Super Hair over the first one. Select a couple of pieces of monofilament and burn the ends to create blob-like balls that replicate eyes. Bind the eyes along the side of the hook.

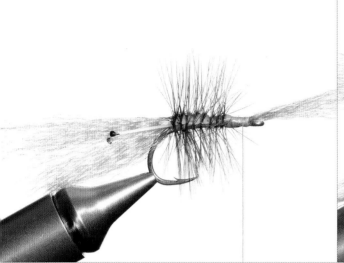 

Step 3

Tie in an orange grizzly hackle and secure two strands of Krystal Flash along the top of the hook shank. Palmer the hackle along the hook, stopping about a quarter of the way back from the hook eye.

Step 4

Trim the top of the hackle fibres. Now select another bunch of Super Hair and tie it in behind the hook eye.

continued >

Step 5

Apply a thin coat of epoxy from the hook eye to just beyond the bend. (As mentioned earlier, this distance is important for two reasons: extending the epoxy beyond the bend will impede hook-ups, and if it extends past the hook eye this may result in the fly tracking off course when retrieved.)

Woolly Bugger

The Woolly Bugger is simplicity in motion. A wet fly used to imitate subaquatic foods, the pattern can be varied to suit different conditions. Try an olive version to imitate a damsel fly nymph, or a tan-coloured one to replicate a yabby. A black Woolly Bugger is preferred for discoloured water, as it provides a better silhouette in murky conditions; if required, a bead head can be added for fishing deeper water. Whatever the colour of the fly, marabou is the material of choice for the tail, delivering an enticing wiggling action.

Cast along drop-offs in lakes or when casting 'blind', and use a slow, steady retrieve once the fly has reached the required depth. In rivers, cast to banks and retrieve back over the drop-off to fish lazing on these edges. Casting across and down, with only occasional twitching, also works well.

Materials

Hook	Kamasan B175 or B830, sizes 8–12	Tail	Black marabou
		Hackle	Black saddle
Thread	Black 6/0	Body	Olive chenille
Weight	Lead wire (optional)		

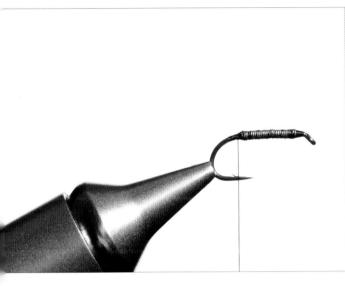

Step 1
(optional: for weighted version)

Start the thread at the hook bend and tie in the lead wire. Advance the thread, wrap the shank in the wire and then tie off. Snip off any excess, then wind the thread to the bend.

Step 2

Tie in a short bunch of marabou. Prepare the chenille by removing a short piece to expose the core thread, then tie in. Tie in the hackle, and advance the thread to just behind the hook eye.

continued >

Step 3

For the body, wrap the hook with chenille and then tie off. Wind the hackle between the layers of chenille, and when you reach the eye, wind the hackle two or three times to form a collar. Tie off, form a neat head, and treat with head cement.

Glossary of terms and tools

BOBBIN HOLDER Tool used to hold the thread spool, allowing precise delivery of the thread under a workable tension.

BODKIN A needle with a large eye, a useful addition to the toolbox (e.g. to apply epoxy or head cement, or to tease out dubbing).

BONEFISH A game fish of tropical waters.

BUCKTAIL HAIR Hair from a deer's tail.

BUTT The base or bottom end.

BUZZER Any insect (e.g. a midge or gnat) that hovers above the surface of the water. Also refers to flies imitating these insect forms.

CADDIS A moth-like aquatic insect.

CHENILLE Furry rope-like material commonly used for making fly bodies, which thus look rather like pipe cleaners. Available in many brands and colours.

CHIRONOMID Scientific name for a midge, a member of the Diptera order of insects. In the pupal stage, they resemble small aquatic worms.

COCK HACKLES The neck feathers of a cockerel.

COLLAR Section of a fly between the head and the body. Usually formed by close turns of a hackle, although some saltwater patterns such as the Pink Thing may use zonker strips wound closely together.

CUL-DE-CANARD Short wispy feathers taken from the rear end (*cul*) of a duck. They add a significant amount of float to a fly, being saturated with oil from the bird's preen gland. Use of floatant on these feathers will actually negate their floating qualities and cause the fly to lose flotation.

DEAD-DRIFT A fly-fishing technique in which the fly is allowed to drift freely along in the current.

DECEIVER PATTERN Any pattern based on Lefty's Deceiver, designed to mimic baitfish.

DEER HAIR Body hair from deer, used in many fly patterns to supply body and flotation.

DRY FLY A fly designed to float on the water's surface.

DUB To apply natural or synthetic hairs to a fly. This is done by applying the hair to the tying thread and rubbing the two between your thumb and forefinger to form a rope, which is then wound onto the hook to form a body. Dubbing loops can also be used in order to produce a finer, tighter rope.

DUBBING NEEDLE A tool for applying dubbing, often serrated so that it catches the dubbing material and makes teasing easier.

DUN The first adult stage (following emergence from the water) of an aquatic insect, especially mayflies.

ELK HAIR Body hair from an elk, which, like deer hair, is used in many fly patterns to supply body and flotation.

EMERGER An aquatic insect in the process of rising to the surface of the water before assuming its adult, flying form. Also refers to flies imitating these insect forms.

FIGURE-OF-EIGHT RETRIEVE A retrieve technique where the fly line is wrapped around the fingers in a figure-of-eight pattern and then bunched in the palm of the hand.

FISH HAIR Synthetic hair used in tying streamers and saltwater flies.

FLASH Any material used to provide sparkle to a fly.

FLASHABOU Trade name for a colourful synthetic filament used for adding flash to many fly patterns.

FLASHBACK A nymph pattern in which a flashy material (such as Flashabou) is used for the wing case.

FLOATANT Any material applied to flies to cause them to float on the surface of the water.

FLOATING LINE A fly-fishing line designed to float on the surface of the water, typically used for trout fishing but also with many applications for saltwater fishing.

FURNACE A red feather with a black centre.

GAPE On a hook, the distance between the point and the section of shank opposite.

GOLDEN PHEASANT A game bird whose crest, neck and wing feathers are used extensively in fly patterns.

GUARD HAIR Longer hairs from the ears of a hare.

HACKLE Soft-stemmed feathers, especially from the neck of a hen or rooster. To prepare a hackle, remove the fibres at the butt of the quill. Hackle pliers are specialised pliers for holding hackle as you wrap it around the hook. They are available in two styles, either fixed or rotating: the rotating version is easier to use. Look also for pliers that will clamp the hackle securely.

HAIR STACKER Tool for aligning tips of fibres used for tying flies. Put the hair in the stacker, tips first, and tap the stacker on the bench top once or twice to align the tips.

HATCH The time when a large number of nymphs or pupas become fully winged insects, often producing frantic feeding activity among trout. Matching the hatch means identifying the insects or baitfish in a particular area and then tying flies to replicate them.

HERL Feathers (usually peacock) with long individual barbules that have short dense fibres.

HOPPER A grasshopper, or a fly that imitates its form.

JUNGLE COCK An Indian game bird whose hackles have distinctive 'eye' markings. It is now an endangered species, but artificial substitutes are available.

KRYSTAL FLASH Trade name for a synthetic stringy material used in many streamer patterns to add flash and colour.

LEADER Section of line used between the fly line and the tippet. Often purchased already tapered, but can be assembled by tying successively smaller diameter sections of monofilament.

LURE Another word for a 'streamer', a fly that represents a small swimming fish.

MARABOU Turkey feather fibres, used extensively for the wings and tails of streamers.

MAYFLY A common aquatic insect which has four life-cycle stages (pupa, larva, dun and spinner) that many fly patterns imitate. Found in moving and still waters, they are a staple food of trout and other fish species.

MONO/MONOFILAMENT A clear, flexible nylon thread which comes in various strengths and diameters.

MYLAR Metallic plastic available in sheet or tube form, used to simulate fish scales on some flies.

NYMPH The immature form of an aquatic insect prior to its emergence from the water. Also refers to flies imitating these insect forms.

PALMER To wind hackle along the body, spacing each wind evenly.

PARACHUTE HACKLE Tying style where hackle is tied (downwards) around a vertical wing post rather than wound around the hook shank.

PATTERN The particular design of material and the position of parts which make up a fly; sometimes called a recipe.

PERMIT A game fish of tropical waters. Also refers to flies used to catch them, such as Del's Merkin.

POLAROIDING The use of polarised glasses to cut through underwater glare.

POPPER Any fly designed to mimic injured or fleeing baitfish.

PUPA The sub-surface larval stage of an aquatic insect.

RETRIEVE The act of pulling in a cast fishing line.

RIB To create body segments and/or to fasten a hackle to the body, using fine wire or other material.

SADDLE FEATHERS Feathers from the back of a chicken, which are longer and have thinner stems than the neck feathers.

SCISSORS You can't have too many in your toolbox. Fine-pointed scissors are used for smaller flies; a larger pair is useful for trimming streamers and saltwater flies to the correct profile; a general-purpose pair can be used for the initial cutting of materials; serrated scissors are also increasingly popular. Keep your scissors sharp.

SCUD Another name for freshwater shrimp.

SEARCHING PATTERN A fly pattern used to seek out fish in known or likely locations, rather than targeting particular fish.

SHOOTING HEAD A fly line with a heavy belly section, usually designed to sink; it may be integrated into the running line, or interchangeable heads are available.

SINKANT Any material used to weight the tip of the fishing line, so that the fly sinks beneath the surface quickly.

SINKING LINE A weighted fly-line, designed to get a wet fly or streamer deeper below the surface.

SLIP A narrow strip of feather.

SPIN To work hair by winding thread two or three times around both the hair and the hook and then pulling tightly on the thread, which causes the hair to flare out and around the hook; the clump of hair should be about the thickness of a pencil.

STREAMER A fly that imitates small swimming fish.

STRIKE To tighten the line and so set the hook when a fish bites, usually by raising the rod tip, lifting the rod, or strip-striking.

STRIP To retrieve a fishing line or to strip it off a reel.

SURFACE FILM The elastic-like film on the surface of water, created by surface tension.

TANDEM FLY A fly consisting of two or more hooks connected by a short length of line.

TAPER The narrowing diameter of a rod from butt to tip, or the narrowing of the end section of a fly line. The rate of taper determines the action of the rod or line.

TERRESTRIAL Any land-based insect, often food for fish.

THORAX The front portion of the body of an insect, to which the wings and legs are attached.

TINSEL Metallic filament used in fly tying to provide flash and colour.

TIPPET The last section of a leader, to which the hook is tied.

VICE Tool for holding the hook securely while you tie a fly. There are many styles and price ranges available, and buying the best you can afford is advisable. The most important feature of a vice is the ability to hold a range of hook sizes securely; some manufacturers supply interchangeable jaws.

WEEDGUARD A length of stout monofilament tied from the bend of the hook to the eye, to produce a curved shape that protects the hook from snagging on weeds, etc.; particularly useful when flies are cast deep into cover.

WET FLY A fly designed to swim beneath the surface.

WHIP-FINISH To secure tied-off thread by creating a loop in it, then wrapping the thread over itself (three to five turns are usually enough) and pulling it back through. A whip-finishing tool makes life easier, though it can look rather daunting to use.

ZONKER STRIP A thin piece of animal skin (e.g. rabbit or fox) with the fur still attached, used as wing material in many flies.

Suppliers and resources | AUSTRALIA

Mail order only: www.motackle.com.au

ACT

Compleat Angler
For store locations, visit
www.compleatangler.com.au
see also New South Wales

NEW SOUTH WALES

Alpine Angler
647 Snowy Mountains Highway
Pine Valley, Cooma
NSW 2630
Ph 02 6452 5538
Email info@alpineangler.com.au
www.alpineangler.com.au

Compleat Angler
For store locations, visit
www.compleatangler.com.au

High Country Outfitters
Shop 8, Nuggets Crossing
Jindabyne
NSW, 2627
Ph 02 6456 2989
Email highfly@acr.net.au
www.highfly.com.au

Otto's Tackle World
74 – 76 Victoria Rd
Drummoyne
NSW 2047
Ph 02 9719 1083
Email fishy.business@bigpond.com
www.fishybusiness.com.au

NORTHERN TERRITORY

Fishing Outdoor World
27 Cavenagh St
Darwin
NT 0801
Ph 08 8981 6398
Email fow@bigpond.com.au

Got One Berrimah
Shop 2 Truck City
Berrimah
NT 0821
Ph 08 8947 2224
Email darwin@gotone.com.au
www.gotone.com.au

QUEENSLAND

Fish Head
Town Centre, Victoria Point
Cnr Redland Bay Rd & Colburn Ave
Victoria Point
Qld 4165
Ph 07 3207 9965
Email duncan@fishhead.com.au
www.fishhead.com.au

Tie 'N' Fly Outfitters
8A Point Cartwright Drive
Buddina
Qld 4575
Ph 07 5444 0611
Email info@tienfly.com
www.tienfly.com

Jones's Tackle
504 Lutwyche Rd
Lutwyche
Qld 4030
Ph 07 3857 5857

Erskine's Tackle World
51 Mulgrave Rd
Cairns
Qld 4870
Ph 07 4051 6099

SOUTH AUSTRALIA

Compleat Angler
For store locations, visit
www.compleatangler.com.au

TASMANIA

Bridges Bros.
71 Bathurst St
Hobart
Tas. 7000
Ph 03 6234 3791

Compleat Angler
For store locations, visit
www.compleatangler.com.au

Essential Fly Fisher
105 York St
Launceston
Tas. 7250
Ph 03 6331 8994
Email essfly@bigpond.net.au
www.essentialflyfisher.com.au

VICTORIA

Armadale Angling
1125 High St
Armadale
Vic. 3143
Ph 03 9822 3896

Aussie Angler
30 Sherbourne Rd
Greensborough
Vic. 3088
Ph 03 0432 1501
Email aussieangling@bigpond.com
www.aussieangler.com.au

Billfisher Tackle
495 Nepean Hwy
Frankston
Vic. 3199
Ph 03 9783 9774
Email billfisher@ozemail.co.au

Compleat Angler
For store locations, visit
www.compleatangler.com.au

J.M. Turville Pty Ltd
126 Franklin St
Melbourne
Vic. 3000
Ph 03 9328 1601

Hook Up Bait and Tackle
718 Burwood Hwy
Ferntree Gully
Vic. 3156
Ph 03 9758 4332
Email hookup@alphalink.com.au
www.hookupfishing.com.au

Goulburn Valley Fly Fishing Centre
Goulburn Valley Highway
Thornton
Vic. 3712
Ph 03 57732513
Email info@goulburnvlyflyfishing.com.au
www.gvffc.com

Ray Long's Tackle World
105 Shannon Ave
Manifiold Heights
Vic. 3218
Ph 03 5222 3257
Email info@raylongtackle.com.au
www.raylongtackle.com.au

WESTERN AUSTRALIA

Sportsmarine Bunbury
113 Victoria St
Bunbury
WA 6230
Ph 08 9721 4961
Email sportsmarine@westnet.com.au

Anglers Anonymous
4/255 Bannister Rd
Canning Vale
WA 6155
Ph 08 9455 2521

Compleat Angler
For storc locations, visit
www.compleatangler.com.au

Flyworld
Suite 2 / 79 Whately Crescent
Bayswater
WA 6933
Ph 1800 066 828
Email info@flyworld.com.au
www.flyworld.com.au

Suppliers and resources | NEW ZEALAND

Online only: www.flyshop.co.nz

NORTH ISLAND

Creel Tackle House
189 Taupahi Rd
Turangi New Zealand
Ph 07 386 7929
Email creel@reap.org.nz

Fish City Hamilton
Cnr Kahikatea Drive & Latham Crt
Frankton, Hamilton
New Zealand
Ph 07 846 6675
Email sales@fishcity.co.nz
www.fishcity.co.nz

Rod and Reel Ltd
20 – 22 Melrose St
Newmarket
Auckland
New Zealand
Ph 09 520 0307
Email sales@rodandreel.co.nz

SOUTH ISLAND

Fishermans' Loft
359 Lincoln Rd
Christchurch
New Zealand
Ph 03 338 3131
Email info@fishermansloft.co.nz
www.fishermansloft.co.nz

Complete Angler
280 Cashel St
Christchurch
New Zealand
Ph 03 366 9885
Email sales@completeangler.co.nz

Index

VIKING

Published by the Penguin Group
Penguin Group (Australia)
250 Camberwell Road, Camberwell, Victoria 3124, Australia
(a division of Pearson Australia Group Pty Ltd)
Penguin Group (USA) Inc.
375 Hudson Street, New York, New York 10014, USA
Penguin Group (Canada)
90 Eglinton Avenue East, Suite 700, Toronto, Canada ON M4P 2Y3
(a division of Pearson Penguin Canada Inc.)
Penguin Books Ltd
80 Strand, London WC2R 0RL England
Penguin Ireland
25 St Stephen's Green, Dublin 2, Ireland
(a division of Penguin Books Ltd)
Penguin Books India Pvt Ltd
11 Community Centre, Panchsheel Park, New Delhi – 110 017, India
Penguin Group (NZ)
Cnr Airborne and Rosedale Roads, Albany, Auckland, New Zealand
(a division of Pearson New Zealand Ltd)
Penguin Books (South Africa) (Pty) Ltd
24 Sturdee Avenue, Rosebank, Johannesburg 2196, South Africa

Penguin Books Ltd, Registered Offices. 80 Strand, London, WC2R 0RL, England

First published by Penguin Group (Australia), 2008

10 9 8 7 6 5 4 3 2 1

Written by Frank O'Leary

Text and photographs copyright © Penguin Group (Australia) 2008

Photography by Maikka Trupp
Cover design by Claire Tice © Penguin Group (Australia)
Text design by Nicholas McGuire © Penguin Group (Australia)
Typeset in Univers by J&M Typesetting
Scanning and separations by Splitting Image Pty Ltd, Clayton, Victoria
Printed in China by 1010 Printing International Limited

Cataloguing information for this book is available from the National Library of Australia

ISBN 9780 670 07083 1

penguin.com.au